Seven Deadly Spirits

Seven Deadly Spirits

*The Message of Revelation's Letters
for Today's Church*

T. Scott Daniels

Baker Academic
a division of Baker Publishing Group
Grand Rapids, Michigan

Published by Baker Academic
a division of Baker Publishing Group
P.O. Box 6287, Grand Rapids, MI 49516-6287
www.bakeracademic.com

Printed in the United States of America

Library of Congress Cataloging-in-Publication Data
Daniels, T. Scott, 1966–
    Seven deadly spirits : the message of Revelation's letters for today's church /
T. Scott Daniels
        p.   cm.
    Includes bibliographical references and indexes.
    ISBN 978-0-8010-3171-7 (pbk.)
        1. Bible. N. T. Revelation I–III—Criticism, interpretation, etc. I. Title.
BS2825.52.D36 2009
228'.06—dc22   2008041702

To Debbie
My Friend and Partner,
And the One Who Keeps
The Angel of Our Home Loving

Contents

Foreword

The book of Revelation is one of my favorite biblical books. I must confess, though, that I have not been inclined to pay much attention to the two chapters in Revelation that contain John's letters to the seven churches of Asia. My typical pattern of reading the book is to start at the first chapter, with John's encounter with the Risen Lord, and then to jump to chapter 4, where the Revelator, having made the dramatic announcement that there is an open door in the heavens, begins to tell us the things that he has been allowed to see and hear. I find the symbolic apocalyptic scenarios fascinating—those wars in the heavens and on earth, and the dragons, beasts, wicked merchants, and corrupt rulers all being ultimately conquered by the Lamb. And then there is the wonderful wrap-up vision of the Holy City in the final chapters.

The letters in chapters 2 and 3 are of a different genre, and I have not been inclined to give them more than a quick, occasional glance. Reading Scott Daniels's wonderful discussion of these letters, however, has forced me to think about why I have neglected the rich biblical materials that he explores in such an illuminating way. In reflecting on my neglect, I realized that I heard a lot of fairly bad sermons on the seven churches in my youth. Those sermons tended to follow one of two lines of interpretation. One line drew directly on the notes in the Scofield Bible, where the seven churches are seen as prophecies about seven different ages of the church—for example, Thyatira was seen as the church era that experienced the rise of the papacy, and Sardis was the Protestant movement of the Reformation era. All of this was treated as a buildup for identifying our own day as the Laodicean age, which signaled an open season for the preachers to condemn the "neither hot nor cold" character of mainline Protestantism, with the warning that God would spit out of his mouth those who conformed to its liberal theological patterns.

The other line of interpretation was a kind of selective moralism. The preacher would pick out a phrase here and there that could launch a sermon on one of his or her pet themes. Under this category, I heard more sermons than I care to think about that drew a parallel between marriages that grow cold and the spiritual syndrome of "losing our first love" in our relationship with the Lord.

And then there was the problem of the "angels" of these churches. The preachers I heard in my youth were strong believers in angels, but in preaching on these particular Revelation texts they would either ignore the angelic presence altogether or make a passing reference to the possibility that God assigns guardian angels to congregations as well as to individual believers. While I puzzled about the ways in which these strategies finessed the topic of angelology, I had no better theory to advance. So I had yet another reason to skip these two chapters.

Scott Daniels has now convinced me that my longstanding neglect of these letters is unfortunate. I have a vague recollection that sometime in the past, when I was working on the Pauline references to "principalities and powers," I came across something—probably in Hendrikus Berkhof or Walter Wink—that suggested to me that there was a link between what Paul was getting at and John's mention of the angels of the seven churches. But I never followed through on the suggestion. Now I can see that this is not only a provocative proposal about how to understand what is going on in Revelation 2 and 3 but also that it makes those letters come alive in profound ways.

And Scott Daniels has exactly what it takes really to make them come alive. He is a solid theologian who is also a gifted preacher and an engaging writer. In this book he weaves together theological scholarship, biblical exposition, and wonderful storytelling. His insightful account of the "seven deadly spirits" has helped me—as I know it will help countless others—hear more clearly what the Spirit has said, and is still saying, to the churches.

Richard J. Mouw
Fuller Theological Seminary

Acknowledgments

This book is the product of many conversations, sermons, and lectures. For several years in the basement of the Department of Theology and Ministry at Southern Nazarene University, my two friends and colleagues, Steve Green and Marty Michelson, helped me grow theologically and biblically through hours of impromptu conversations in which we deliberated over most of the American church's major problems. I don't miss grading term papers and final exams, but I do miss those conversations. It was in one such conversation with Steve that the primary idea for this book arose, and he graciously allowed me to be the one to run with the idea.

A couple of years later, the idea that churches have a collective spirit or essence that the Revelator refers to as an "angel" turned into a sermon series that the great congregation at Richardson Church of the Nazarene patiently endured and helped shape. The wonderful members of First Church of the Nazarene of Pasadena also have been so kind in not only attending lectures on the seven churches but also participating in a video shoot for lessons that go along with the book. I want to thank the people of PazNaz for being more than just hearers of the Word; they have continued to work with the pastoral leadership to allow the Spirit to transform the angel of our church.

I certainly want to thank Bob Hosack, Jeffery Wittung, and Baker Academic for being patient with all our many family transitions and

13

seeing the project through to completion. It was also incredibly kind of my longtime friend and mentor, Dr. Richard Mouw, to write the foreword for the book.

But most of all I want to thank Debbie, Caleb, Noah, Jonah, and Sophie for loving me, cheering me on, and giving me the space to finish this work. This book is dedicated to my wife, Debbie, who is the real secret to why the ethos, spirit, or angel of our home is a happy and loving one.

Introduction

To the Angel, Write . . .

The envelope marked "confidential" was waiting for us when we got home.

My wife and I had just returned from a five-day interview session with a church that was considering me as a candidate to be their senior pastor. Inside the envelope was a three-page, typed, single-spaced letter from a former member of the congregation we had just interviewed with, rehearsing the last ten years of sins the church—in this parishioner's mind—had committed against God and against each other. The letter began something like this: "I hear that you are considering becoming pastor at . . . . I don't have any idea what has possessed you or what crazy thoughts you must be thinking! That church is a sinful, evil, pastor killer. No one can pastor that church and survive." The letter ended by giving me contact information for the four most recent senior pastors of the church and encouraging me to hear their stories and then run for my life.

My guess is that letters such as the one I received could be written, and probably are being written, about many congregations in North America today. I know few pastors who regard the ministry as a safe occupation anymore. Leading the church has never been an easy calling—as Paul's letters to the Corinthian church attest—but there does seem to be an especially toxic mix of cultural, economic, and spiritual influences that make leadership in the church today a sometimes less-than-desirable life pursuit. Consumerism, materialism, sensuality, militarism, personal preferences in style of worship, the rise of technology, and the politicization of the church are just a few examples on a long list of challenges facing pastors, pastoral staff, and lay leaders.

This book rose out of a seemingly minute biblical discovery that radically changed some basic assumptions for me as a pastor. This discovery occurred as I was wrestling with what appeared at the time to be a somewhat marginal question while preparing for a sermon series on the book of Revelation. Why, I wondered, did John, in chapters 2 and 3 of his Revelation, address the seven letters to the seven churches in Asia to the *angels* of those particular churches? The exegesis of the messages contained in the letters took up the bulk of my study time, but I could not shake the question of the angels. Why write to angels?

I sought the help of a respected friend and scholar who not only gave me the seminal insight for this book but also pointed me to Hendrikus Berkhof's *Christ and the Powers*,[1] which then led me to Walter Wink's powerful four-part series on "the powers": *Naming the Powers, Unmasking the Powers, Engaging the Powers,* and *When the Powers Fall.*[2] Berkhof and Wink's understanding of what the Scriptures name as "principalities and powers" brought to my mind the work of one of my former professors—Nancey Murphy—on the nature of human beings. In her work on the relationship between the body and soul, Murphy argues for what she calls "non-reductive physicalism,"[3] which means, in essence, that a person cannot be reduced to the physical matter that makes up the body nor can a person be reduced to a spiritual essence that is completely separate from the physical. To put it simply, Murphy argues that people are made of many physical parts, but when those parts are all put together something more—something spiritual—emerges. People are always more than the sum of their parts.

Reading the work of Berkhof, Wink, and Murphy in conjunction with several recent commentaries on Revelation led me to the basic conviction that forms the thesis of this book. It is my conviction that John the Revelator[4] writes to the angels of the churches because he recognizes something profound and complex about the way churches are formed as communities. The seven churches of Asia—like all communal bodies—are more than the sum of the individuals that make up that community. Communities, like the individual persons from which they are formed, take on a kind of spirit, personality, or "life of their own" that becomes greater than the sum of their physical parts. The seven angels of the churches, to whom John writes, are neither disconnected spiritual beings nor merely a colorful way of describing nonexistent realities. Instead, the term "angel" signifies the very real ethos or communal essence that either gives life to or works at destroying the spiritual fabric of the very community that gave birth to it.

At first this may seem like a relatively insignificant insight, but it is an idea that has significantly altered the way I approach leadership in the church. I am now convinced that churches, because they are a communal body, have an essence or collective spirit that is at work either aiding or hindering the life-giving work of the Spirit of God. Changing the destructive aspects of this communal spirit requires more than simply preaching the right sermon, discovering the latest ministry program, or even pruning a handful of contentious people from the community; rather, transformation of a church requires naming, unmasking, and calling to repentance the spirit or ethos that holds a church captive. I believe that what is required today for effective church leadership can only be described as a kind of spiritual warfare.

I will confess that I have struggled in writing this book. I am a very empirical person by nature and by education. The words "angels," "spirits," or "spiritual warfare" do not make their way into my vocabulary with great frequency. One of my fears even mentioning angels or spirits is that people will associate what I am writing with some form of hyperspirituality. It is certainly my hope and belief that brothers and sisters in Christ with a more charismatic worldview than my own will receive help and insight from this study, but I am writing primarily to those who, like me, tend toward empiricism. Empiricists, because they tend to focus only on the material or physical aspects of the church, tend to think that if they just work a little harder, plan a little smarter, or tinker with the structure a bit, they will get better results. Although hard work and the development of church programs certainly have their place, I am increasingly convinced that leaders of communities, especially those who lead deeply committed and connected communities like churches, wrestle with systems and structures—principalities and powers, to borrow a phrase from Paul—that require them to approach their leadership differently.

It is my hope that this book will be helpful for pastors, administrators, lay leaders, and students preparing for ministry who long to see the community of individuals called the church transformed into the body of Christ glorifying God in the world. In particular, I hope that the insights of this study will be helpful to those agents of change who are frustrated with a programmatic approach to transformation. I will warn you at the beginning that this book does not offer the reader a new program for ministry. My experience growing up in the parsonage, observing churches from a distance, and now trying to lead a congregation has made me realize that there is no fail-proof, life-changing, five-step strategy that will transform every church. It is my observation that, like David trying to fight in Saul's armor, what works in one congregation usually fails miserably in another. This is a book for those who are burned out on seminars and are ready to do battle with the communal attitudes and collective spirits that hold the church back from fully bringing glory to its Lord despite our best efforts at programmatic alteration and implementation.

Before getting into the content of each letter, I want to first reflect on how the book of Revelation ought to be read and interpreted and where the seven letters fit in the overall framework of John's apocalyptic letter. Second, I want to describe in more detail what I have simply introduced as the corporate or emerging nature of the angels or spirits of the seven churches. And finally, I want to examine why there are *seven* letters and how the seven spirits, or collective attitudes, addressed by the Revelator make their appearances in the church today.

Reading Revelation

I think my favorite ride at Disneyland is the Haunted Mansion. Something about hitchhiking ghosts and singing busts in a cemetery captures my imagination. One of the best sections of the mansion is the spooky portrait gallery one walks into after leaving the stretching room with no windows and no doors. Each eerie painting that hangs on the wall presents something beautiful initially—the portrait of an elegant woman, a powerful ship, or a general on horseback—but upon second look one realizes that the woman is now a Medusa-like hag, the ship has become a phantom ghost-ship, and the general has been transformed into a skeletal apparition. The mystery of the mansion's gallery is the ability to see behind and beyond the beauty to discover what lies beneath.

The book of Revelation has been read and interpreted in many different ways. It has often been viewed as a cloudy and mysterious work by John the Apostle, filled with veiled predictions about the future. Using various interpretive keys, many theologians, scholars, and pastors have worked out great systems and charts in an attempt to name the political forces of evil that will oppress the church, to identify the beast or beasts who will rise to power, and most importantly, to predict the time and date of Christ's second advent. Others have grown so frustrated by the murkiness of the Revelator's apocalyptic images that they have essentially abandoned the study of the book altogether. I remember a professor of mine once saying, "The study of John's Apocalypse has been the *least* helpful discipline in the history of Christianity."

I believe the purpose of this great and awesome revealed word to the early church was not to give the church the key to predict the future but to give the followers of Christ in the first century the ability to view from the perspective of the divine the culture that surrounded them. Like the pictures in the Haunted Mansion that reveal their hidden ugliness when viewed from another angle, the language of Revelation serves as a pair of linguistic glasses that we place over our spiritual eyes to see clearly the nature of the principalities and powers. Like the majority of their friends and neighbors, when the first-century believers looked at Rome—the nation that had established the *Pax Romana*—they saw an alluring goddess (Roma) of power and might, fame and prestige, health and wealth that offered the cup of life to its citizens and to all who would come and worship it. When one looks again, however, this time through the apocalyptic language of the

[handwritten top margin: That only in God the Father – God the Son & God the Holy Spirit allows us help us become overcomers. His Glory + Adoration]

[handwritten left margin: for each of our lives to be / are introduced to them difference / memories)]

Revelator, one discovers that the principality and power that claims to be a goddess is instead "the great whore who corrupted the earth with her fornication" (Rev. 19:2), who does not hold the cup of life but rather "a golden cup full of abominations and the impurities of her fornication" (17:4).

The name "Babylon" is central to the Revelator's apocalyptic pair of linguistic glasses. The primary force that opposes the gospel in John's vision from Patmos is not the beast or the Antichrist but the principality and power he names Babylon. The story of God's people has always been juxtaposed to the counterstory of a particular power or *empire*. In the days of Moses, Egypt enslaved and oppressed the children of Jacob. The Canaanites, Philistines, and other dangerous nations threatened Israel with the sword and with the allure of the Baals as they tried to make their way in the Promised Land. The powerful and violent nation of Assyria captured the northern nation of Ephraim (Israel) and forced the people to relocate. In 587 BCE, Babylon, led by King Nebuchadnezzar, defeated the southern nation of Judah, utterly destroyed Jerusalem and the temple, and led the young and gifted into exile.

Babylon holds a special place in the great and populated pantheon of Jewish oppressors and captors, especially for the biblical prophets. Particularly in the book of Daniel, the reader discovers that the primary problem of Israel's second great exile was that life in Babylon wasn't nearly as oppressive as their days of slavery in Egypt. Egypt violently oppressed the Israelites. Although many people died at the hand of Pharaoh, the children of Israel were not invited or tempted to become Egyptians. The distinct problem of the Babylonian exile was that the culture of Babylon gave enough freedom and offered enough wealth and power to their Israelite and Judean captives that the greatest risk the people faced was not slavery and oppression but that their children would become Babylonians. In fact, when we read the famous stories of the Hebrew children facing the fiery furnace, rather than bowing to the king and Daniel accepting the lions' den rather than accepting restrictions to his faith, we realize that their faith was demonstrated in their ability to resist the lure of the Babylonian empire and *not* be assimilated into or be conformed to the culture.

In the opening story of Daniel (Dan. 1:3–21), the strong and bright of Judah are invited to sit at King Nebuchadnezzar's table and eat the sumptuous food offered to the king's best men. This oppression is hardly the back-breaking labor of trying to make bricks without straw. The Hebrew children, however, understand that sitting at Nebuchadnezzar's table will essentially make them the king's rather than Yahweh's children. Rather than eat at the table, bow to the idol, or obey the codes against prayer, the exemplary young leaders—Shadrach, Meshach, Abednego, and Daniel—resist the allure of the Babylonian empire while enduring the risk and cost of nonconformity.

Situated in another empire, Rome, John the Revelator recognizes that the primary challenge his brothers and sisters in the early church face is not just sporadic persecution but the constant lure to compromise with their new Babylon. Like Shadrach, Meshach, Abednego, and Daniel before them, the first-century Christians must constantly be alert to the ways the empire is pressing them into its mold. The book of Revelation gives the early church the language—the linguistic glasses if you will—to see that the goddess Roma (the spiritual embodiment of the power of Rome) will not give them the abundant life she promises; instead, like Babylon she will lure them into a variety of compromises that will conform them to her values and rob them of the abundant and eternal life they have received and are experiencing through the Lamb.5

I am strongly convinced that it is inappropriate to interpret Revelation as a hidden map to future events. Certainly the hope of God's future is a central, if not *the* central, supposition of John's apocalyptic message to the early church. But instead of providing early-church believers with a hidden map to future events that lay at least two thousand years beyond their own day, John's inspired message to the early church is meant to enliven in them, in the midst of persecution and chaos, faith that God indeed has the final word in creation and will redeem all things and reconcile the creation to himself in his time.

The letters to the seven Asian churches are central to this message. Although the letters found in chapters 2 and 3 are very different in form and style from the spectacular vision that is articulated in the chapters that follow, they are an integral part of the entire message of Revelation. The work of Revelation in its fullness is designed to prod the early church to patiently endure the persecution and struggles coming from within and without and to be prepared for the high cost of discipleship in a culture antithetical to the ideals of the gospel. Like the Hebrew children who chose obedience to Yahweh over service to Nebuchadnezzar, believers will need to diligently hold on to their faith and be prepared for whatever sacrifice may be necessary in the conflict between Christ and caesar.

The Revelator recognizes that it takes a special set of skills to live a faithful Christian life in caesar's Babylon. Certainly the "visible caesar" represents the continual threat of violence and persecution inflicted on those who seem suspicious to the status quo because of their perceived disloyalties. The larger letter of Revelation, and the letters within the letter, contains many references to endurance, long-suffering, and hope beyond physical death, but John seems equally to recognize the threat of the "hidden caesar" that invites us to compromise. To find caesar in all his hiding places requires the believer to see the world apocalyptically. The spiritual survival of the early Christians depended on their ability to *not* see Rome as the eternal city but to see her as another Babylon on the way to implosion and collapse (Rev. 19). Followers of Christ cannot view the economics of the empire as "just business"; rather, they must have the insight to see it as the trap and lure of the beast. Disciples, who are committed to overcoming evil with good, must not view political and military power as a necessary means to a peaceful end, but they must be able to recognize in caesar's chariots and horses the never-ending cycle of the principalities and powers' attempts to overcome coercive power with more coercive power and to stop violence through the use of greater violence.

Beyond imploring the early church to endure difficulty, the seven letters and the entire book of Revelation also contain a powerful message to be aware of the ways in which the church is profoundly shaped and "conformed to this world" (Rom. 12:2). Each church is caught in a tug-of-war between Christ and its surrounding culture. In each letter, the church is called by the one "who walks among the seven golden lampstands" (Rev. 2:1) to "listen to what the Spirit is saying to the churches" (2:7) and to "conquer" or overcome the forces that are keeping it from fulfilling its divine purpose and character. To summarize in the words of Craig Koester, "Despite their differences, all the congregations were alike in that they were subject to currents that threatened to undermine their commitments, whether blatantly through persecution, or more subtly through the erosion of the basis of their faith."[6]

And so we must return to the question of why these letters are addressed to the angel of each church. What is the significance of the angels?

To the Angel . . .

There are generally three possibilities for interpreting John's use of the term *angel*: materialistic, spiritualistic, or what I will describe as emergent.

The materialistic interpretation suggests that the term *angel* refers to a person.[7] The word for angel in the Greek is *aggelos*, or *angelos*, which literally means "messenger." This has led some commentators to argue that it is simply the overseer or pastor of each local church who is addressed. However, using *angel* in this way would be rather surprising given that it is not used in this way in any other New Testament context and because elsewhere in Revelation *angel* is always used to describe a heavenly being.[8] It would also seem strange that a letter clearly intended to be read in the communal worship of the congregation would be addressed solely to a particular individual.

A second interpretive possibility is to read *angel* in a spiritualistic manner. *Aggelos* could be interpreted literally: an angel, a disembodied spiritual being mysteriously connected or assigned to a particular congregation.[9] Jewish and Christian literature of the day often spoke of guardian angels assigned to nature, nations, cities, families, and persons. It is possible that John's use of the term is an extension of this practice.[10] Again, the way the letter was intended to be read is problematic for this interpretation. Although addressed to an angel, it seems apparent that these letters were meant to be read corporately to the members of the congregations within the practice of worship, and it also seems apparent that either the affirmation of faithfulness or the call to repentance is intended to be received not by a disembodied spiritual being but by the flesh-and-blood members of the church. In other words, it does not seem logical to believe that there is a guardian angel of Laodicea that is causing the members of the church to be lukewarm; rather, it is much more likely that the people who make up the church of Laodicea have, in their life together, formed a spirit of lukewarmness that the Spirit of God wishes would become either hot or cold.

This leads me to the third possibility and back to the interpretation that will be the foundational assumption for all that follows. I believe the angel of each church is not a leader or another material individual within the church or a purely spiritual entity guarding, keeping, and possessing the church without its knowledge; the angel is not separate from the congregation but rather *emerges* from its corporate life, representing and shaping its life in community. Walter Wink describes it this way:

> It would appear that the angel is not something separate from the congregation, but must somehow represent it as a totality. Through the angel, the community seems to step forth as a single collective entity or Gestalt. But the fact that the angel is actually addressed suggests that it is more than a mere personification of the church, but the actual spirituality of the congregation as a single entity. The angel would then exist in, with, and under the material expressions of the church's life as its interiority. As the corporate personality or felt sense of the whole, the angel of the church would have no separate existence apart from the people. But the converse would be equally true: the people would have no unity apart from the angel.[11]

If this understanding of the angels of the churches is indeed proper, then John's use of this terminology demonstrates that he has recognized a profound reality within the lives of the churches. John perceives that there is an "ethos" or "spirit" of each congregation that is more than simply the sum of its parts.[12] In this view, the angel is a kind of corporate personality created and formed by the members of the church and the surrounding culture but now operating in such a way that it in turn shapes, reinforces, and holds the collective life of that congregation in its grasp.[13]

For the sake of clarification, it might be helpful to use as a brief comparison some current work being done in the area of the philosophy of personhood. In fact, I am borrowing the word "emergent" from a group of theorists who describe themselves as "emergentist."[14] There has been a longstanding debate in the philosophy of personhood concerning the nature of the body and the soul and their relationship to each other. Similar to the possible ways to interpret the angels of the churches, the arguments about the relationship of body and soul fall roughly into the same three categories: materialistic, spiritualistic (or dualistic), and emergent.

A materialist view of the human person could also be described as a reductive view. The materialist perspective reduces every aspect of the human person to the basic corporeal matter of the body and "seeks to explain us entirely in terms of the behavior of the physical stuff of which we are made."[15] For the materialist, there is no such thing as the human soul per se, and thus the possibility for human freedom is highly questioned because all behavior can be explained as processes—albeit complex processes—of cause and effect.

On the other extreme, a spiritualistic or dualistic view holds that "a human person consists of a body somehow joined to a soul that is fundamentally totally different from the body and bears no necessary relation to it."[16] In other words, dualism believes that people are made up of two very distinct parts: the body and the soul. Although there is some communication between these two entities while they are combined as a living person, they are considered to be very distinct in their essence. Most forms of dualism degrade the body as the lower of these two entities and elevate the soul as the true spiritual essence of a person.

This dualistic view has faced serious philosophical problems dating back to Descartes' inability to describe how the two separate substances of mind (soul) and body could be connected, communicate, and influence each other. This view is also under assault by current work in the philosophies of science and psychology. Here there is a recognition of the intimate link between the material substance of the body and nervous system (the brain in particular) and the personality and selfhood of a person. So while materialism seems to have "little to offer . . . dualism [is] almost equally perplexing."[17]

Between these two extremes are several varieties of an emergent theory. This theory essentially argues that when all the parts of the human person are assembled, a new property emerges that is most frequently described as "soul" or "mind." William Hasker defines emergence this way:

> The core idea of emergence is that, when elements of a certain sort are assembled in the right way, something new comes into being, something that was not there before. The new thing is not just a rearrangement of what was there before, but neither is it something dropped into the situation from the outside. It "emerges," comes into being, through the operation of the constituent elements, yet the new thing is something different and often surprising; we would not have expected it before it appeared. . . . You will think of this new element not as something "added from the outside" but as something that arises somehow out of the original constituents of the situation.[18]

Thus the fundamental idea of emergence is that when a certain configuration of the brain and the nervous system are put together, a new entity emerges—namely, the mind or soul of a person.

In this view, the mind or soul is a new substance or thing. Hasker likens it to the relationship between a magnet and its magnetic field. Although dependent on the magnet for its existence, the field the magnet produces is—in a very real sense—a "thing" in itself. For emergentists, the mind or soul is not made of the physical and chemical stuff of which the brain is composed, though it crucially depends on the matter of the brain for both its existence and its sustenance. It is the emerging conscious mind that thinks and reasons and feels emotions and makes decisions. This mind or soul that has now emerged is the core of what we mean when we think about a person.

Like emergentists who argue concerning human persons that, given a particular complex arrangement, something new and previously nonexistent appears, Wink interprets the angels of the churches as those entities that emerge from the collective lives of the various members of the churches. "They are the visible and invisible aspects of a single corporate reality. . . . The angel gathers up into a single whole all the aspirations and grudges, hopes and vendettas, fidelity and unfaithfulness of a given community of believers, and lays it all before God for judgment, correction, and healing."[19]

I want to argue in this book that churches have corporate personalities or systemic spirits—angels—that are formed out of the mixture of all their parts, both personal and cultural. That corporate identity takes on a life of its own and shapes the attitude, spiritual climate, and future trajectory of that church. Although this spirit or ethos is dependent on the members of the church for its life—for they birthed it into existence—this angel has now emerged in such a way that it influences and shapes the corporate life of the church for good or for evil. In this way Paul is correct: "Our struggle is not against enemies of blood and flesh, but against . . . the spiritual forces of evil" (Eph. 6:12).

How are these angels formed? What forces come together to create the angels of the churches? Wink suggests six.[20] The first is the architecture and ambiance of a church. Buildings, Wink argues, are both an explicit statement about the values, prestige, and class of a community and a force that continues to shape those values into the future. Economic and educational levels are a second force that determines the spirit of a church. Power structures, leadership styles, theological orientations, and attitudes toward authority are a third formational force. The fourth force Wink identifies is the way a congregation handles conflict. Fifth, the nature of liturgy or corporate worship in the church and the way in which spiritual growth is developed and assessed contributes to the emergence of the church's angel. And finally, Wink argues that the church's perception of itself and its community profoundly shapes its collective identity. According to Wink, the following questions are vital to how the spirit or angel of a church is formed:

> How does the congregation see itself? How do others see it? Does membership confer status, or does it indicate a high level of commitment to mission? Is the church inner- or outer-directed? Is it related to its neighborhood or the larger community? Is it self-engrossed, or engaged in struggles for social justice and global peace? Is it evangelistic or nurturing, or both? Is it on speaking terms with its angel and fired by a sense of its divine vocation, or is it a country club, or a haven against the chill of rapid social change? What is the place of

spirituality, or prayer and meditation, of the inner journey? Is it easy
to "get on board," to become drawn into the life of the group? What
about its history, its traditions, its annual celebrations, its invariant
money-raisers and teas? Who have been its heroes and its villains, and
what are the skeletons in its closet?[21]

These sources and influences of the collective spirit of the church
could perhaps go on without end, for in the same way that we experience the mystery and amazement that comes as we encounter the
powers that emerge to form the mind, personality, or soul of a person
when the proper configuration of matter is achieved, there is an equal
complexity to the organizational psychology and corporate spirit of
a collection of individuals called the church.

It is therefore the thesis of this study that real change takes place in
the church not simply by altering the visible structures of the institution,
such as changing pastoral staff, instituting new programs, or modifying
the style of worship, but by altering the spirit or the core essence of
the entity as a whole. I want to be very clear: those who would seek to
change the church must change things that are seen. The deadly spirits
that we will explore cannot be changed without the people, structures,
and methods of the church changing, but I am convinced that the
genius of the letters in Revelation is John's underlying recognition
that complete change cannot occur without naming, describing, and
calling to account the collective spirit of the church.

Seven Angels

Before I turn to the particular letters and begin to wrestle with the deadly
spirits revealed in them, perhaps a word about the number of letters and
angels is needed. There are indeed seven letters addressed to the seven
churches in chapters 2 and 3 of Revelation. Why *seven* letters? Why
seven churches? Is there some significance to this number? It may be that
these seven churches were simply the seven most significant churches in
Asia or the seven churches existing in the seven most significant cities.
It may be that these were the seven churches with which John had the
closest emotional and spiritual ties, and thus it is just incidental that

the number turned out to be seven. It is more likely, however, that the number seven is meant to be understood as a significant symbol.

Seven is used elsewhere by the Revelator to number spirits, lamps, lampstands, stars, seals, horns and eyes on the Lamb, trumpets, thunders, crowns, heads on a beast, plagues, golden bowls, hills, and kings. In each of these references it is apparent that the number seven is to be taken as a symbolic number representing completeness or fullness. Just as the days of creation were completed with the seventh day, the seven horns and eyes on the Lamb represent the idea that Christ, the Lion who is the Lamb, has complete power (seven horns) and has complete wisdom and insight into all things (seven eyes).[22] If, then, seven is to be taken as the number signifying completion, then these seven letters are addressed not just to seven particular congregations but to the entire or complete church. These proclamations given to the seven Asian churches in their particularity also serve as messages for the church universal.

It has become my conviction that these seven letters address general attitudes or spirits that continue to be at work in the church today. The more I studied and tried to interpret these seven particular letters, the more I began to see correlations between the concerns John had for these seven churches and the kinds of concerns that I discern in the contemporary church. I don't believe that there are only seven problems, seven attitudes, or seven deadly spirits that affect the church today, but these seven angels or deadly spirits represent key areas of struggle that were destructive in the early church and continue to be damaging to contemporary congregations.

Every church has its own unique collective spirit. If my theory about the angels of the churches in Revelation is correct, then the spirit that emerges from a congregation is formed by a unique combination of human action, institutional history, and cultural influence. The corporate spirit that emerges in every church captures the hopes, fears, and horizons of imagination for a congregation. Again, that spirit is more than the collection of individual attitudes; it is shaped by leaders of the past, but it also shaped them. It is formed in the context of national and local cultures, but it also interprets those same cultures. It lives in the stories that are told in public gatherings and in the stories that are whispered in secret hallways. It is spiritual, but it is also physical. It is corporate, and yet it dwells within the hearts of individuals. Therefore, it requires pragmatic plans of action, but it also requires insights and strategies of attack that can only be described as a type of spiritual warfare. It requires the complexity of the body of Christ—a body that is more than the sum of its parts—naming, evaluating, and calling to repentance its destructive spirit.

The chapters that follow take a hard exegetical look at each letter and each church, locating each church within its social context, recognizing the influence of the culture within and without, and naming the spirit that holds each captive. My guess is that no contemporary church will be reflected precisely in any singular letter. It is more likely that churches are diverse mixtures of two or three of the spirits described by the Revelator.

I am aware that of the seven letters located in Revelation 2 and 3, five of the letters are negative (or call for repentance) and two are affirming. For the sake of consistency, I have used the two positive letters to imagine what the opposite of the "good angel" or spirit would be and what the church would look like that has allowed such a spirit to emerge from its corporate life.

Chapter 1 deals with the angel of Ephesus, an angel I call *the spirit of boundary keeping*. In Ephesus we discover a church faced with rapid change that, in the midst of standing for what is right, has lost its ability to love one another.

The second chapter deals with Smyrna and *the spirit of consumerism*. The people of the church in Smyrna were able to persist in the midst of great persecution and tribulation despite the city's history of frequent destruction. I contrast this with the pervasive spirit of consumption that makes covenant and commitment a very difficult quality to find in the contemporary body of Christ.

Pergamum's *spirit of accommodation* is described in chapter 3. In this chapter I look at the struggle of the contemporary church with the issue of power. This happens in both our struggle not to misuse power from within and our tendency to participate in and glorify cycles of power outside the church.

Chapter 4 explores the church in Thyatira and *the spirit of privatized faith*. The early church struggled with the implications of the common Greek philosophical perspective of the day that divided the spirit or soul from the body. If the soul is separate from the body, as some thought, then perhaps we can serve God—who is Spirit—with our spirits and be free to do whatever we like with our bodies. The angel of privatized faith—separating the spiritual from the secular—deeply damages the church and its witness in the world.

The fifth chapter details the angel of Sardis, *the spirit of apathetic faith*. Like Sardis, in our prosperous ease and apathy, it is possible for a church to have the appearance of being alive but from Christ's perspective be dead.

Chapter 6 again deals with a reversal. The angel of the church in Philadelphia is held in esteem because of its "open door." The Philadelphians are praised in this letter because they had turned their challenges into opportunities, or open doors, for the gospel. I look at the opposite of this angel to describe *the spirit of fear* that afflicts many contemporary congregations. Rather than confronting the challenges of contemporary life—especially the challenge of diversity—the church seems to turn in on itself, celebrate its safe homogeneity, and close its doors to the possibilities for new life all around.

The final chapter on the deadly spirits—chapter 7—explores the letter that is perhaps the most familiar to believers. Although many know that Laodicea is chided by the Lord for being lukewarm, I explore here *the spirit of self-sufficiency*. The chapter describes the lukewarmness of Laodicea as symptomatic of a congregation that has cut itself off from the life-giving source of the Lord, who stands at the door and knocks, because it has found the answers to its problems from within itself.

In the concluding chapter I briefly describe a method transformational leaders can use in addressing the deadly spirits that bind the church. I describe what it means to name the spirit of the church, call that spirit to repentance, and then embody new practices in community that can transform the spirit from spiritually deadly to spiritually life giving. In particular, I discuss what it might mean for the church to have the "ears to hear what the Spirit is saying" as we learn to live out the Scriptures together in community. As the church learns to read and embody Scripture in community, we also learn to see and resist the powers—the deadly spirits—that hold us captive.

I'm sure that what is true of the church is also true of other institutions. Microsoft has a unique angel that separates it from other computer software companies. Certainly both consistently winning and perennially losing athletic organizations have an ethos—a team spirit—that other organizations want to either emulate or avoid. City, state, and national governments and citizenry are subject to the collective consciousness of their locations and histories, but I am convinced churches are still distinctive in dealing with their angels. For unlike IBM, the Los Angeles Lakers, or the United States of America, the church is uniquely called by God to be his holy nation and his royal priesthood in the world. If the Yankees miss the playoffs for a decade, most of life will continue on as normal, but if the church fails to be God's image and reflection in the world, the salt and light of the kingdom of hope will go missing.

The task of identifying and battling the deadly spirits is critical for the sake of the kingdom, but it is important to recognize that our hope in transforming the communal spirit of the contemporary church from a destroyer to a life giver is not ultimately in our hands. In the end, the role of transformation belongs to the one who is "the first and the last, and the living one" (Rev. 1:17–18). The words of warning and praise to the churches are the words of the risen Christ. He is the one "who holds the seven stars in his right hand, who walks among the seven golden lampstands" (2:1).

By the way, my wife and I did accept the call to the "pastor-killing" congregation. We have been serving there only for a handful of years, but we're certainly not dead yet. In fact, we seem to be learning together as a congregation to name the deadly spirit that has kept us from all that God wants to do in and through us. It is taking some of the conventional weapons of spiritual warfare—prayer, preaching, confession, and the like—to accomplish this task, but I believe that with God's help we are learning to name our angel and call it to repentance. There is a very good chance that our deadly spirit looks very much like some combination of the angels that John describes as holding sway over the great Asian churches. Naming and transforming the spirits that damage the church is not easy. As each of the letters reminds us, "Let anyone who has an ear listen to what the Spirit is saying to the churches" (2:7).

1

Ephesus

The Spirit of Boundary Keeping

"To the angel of the church in Ephesus write: . . . I know that you cannot tolerate evildoers. . . . But I have this against you, that you have abandoned the love you had at first."

My first opportunity to preach after I graduated from college was at a youth camp in the Northwest. I was responsible for speaking ten times over six days. I accepted the invitation knowing I had only two sermons from college in my files. I outlined a series on the life of King David that I thought would work well, but I was still missing a "hook." During my senior year of college a special speaker had come for a week-long revival, and at the beginning of each service he had read a different children's book as a way of introducing the message. The books were repetitive and funny and drew even a culturally cool college crowd into the moment, so I decided I would borrow his idea and use a children's book as a lead-in to each of my camp messages.

I spent nearly a day and a half at the local bookstore searching through book after book for funny, repetitive stories that would in some way or another tie in with the life of David. One of my favorite children's authors is Robert Munsch, well known for his book *I'll Love You Forever*. Like *Forever*, most of Munsch's books are repetitive, quirky in their humor, and meaningful. Several of the books I chose to use were authored by him, including one titled *Thomas' Snowsuit*. The book is about a young boy named Thomas who lives in Minnesota, where children often need to wear snowsuits. Thomas's mother buys him a brown snowsuit that he refuses to wear because he believes it is too ugly. Each time she tries to get him to wear it he says, "NOOO!" Thomas and his mother get into a huge wrestling match, but the mother finally succeeds in getting Thomas into his snowsuit, and he heads to school.

When it is time for recess at school, the teacher asks Thomas to please put on his snowsuit. Thomas says, "NOOO!" Again she asks, but Thomas says, "NOOO!" Thomas and the teacher then get into a wrestling match, but rather than ending up in his snowsuit, Thomas ends up in the teacher's dress and the teacher ends up wearing nothing but her underwear. The principal of the school gets involved, but rather than helping the situation, he increases the chaos by repeatedly adding another person to the wrestling match. Each character alternately winds up either in another person's clothing or in his or her underwear. Finally, some friends call Thomas to come outside and play. Immediately he jumps into his snowsuit and heads out for recess, leaving the teacher in the principal's suit and the principal in the teacher's dress. The book ends with the principal moving to Arizona where children do not wear snowsuits.

I planned to use the book to introduce the Wednesday night message on the rebellious life of David's son Absalom and how his life became not only a stumbling block to others but also ultimately destructive to himself. Before the service, I noticed that a very conservative-looking family, who had not been part of the camp during the week, had come to visit that evening. I found out later that they had brought their daughter to be part of the mid-week service and hear the guest speaker but that they had not allowed her to be part of the camp because the camp leaders were allowing the teenage boys and girls to swim together in the lake.

The beginning of the message was going well. I was reading *Thomas' Snowsuit* and the teens were saying "NOOO!" in unison with Thomas each time he refused to put on his snowsuit. When I got to the part where the teacher and Thomas end up for a time in their underwear, I noticed that someone was moving off to my left, but I paid little attention to them. I looked up from my book just in time to see the mother of the visiting family sprinting across the platform. In a fit of righteous indignation, she grabbed the book out of my hands and shouted, "That is quite enough!" Then she walked off with the book under her arm and headed for the exit.

I was obviously stunned and wasn't quite sure how to go on. The only person more stunned than me was the camp director, who was sitting in the front row with his mouth open, not quite sure what had just happened. I broke the tension by saying, "I had planned to speak to you tonight about being a stumbling block, but apparently I have already been one. I suppose we should pray." I don't remember what I prayed, but I remember thinking, "I haven't even had a ministry career yet, and I have already ruined it." When I got done praying I tried to carry on with the message. I noticed that the camp director was no longer in his seat. I could see him through the glass doors in the back arguing with the woman who had taken my book. They were both very angry. Their heated argument continued until well after my message was over. When the service concluded, I went outside to try to make peace (and to try to get my book back). I apologized as genuinely as I knew how for offending her. Instead of accepting my apology, she began to accuse me of bringing pornography, illicit sexuality, and corruption into the house of God.

There is much more to the story, but thankfully my career in ministry wasn't destroyed (and I did get my book back). There are many thoughts—not all of them holy—that come to mind when I think of that night, but one thing I can never quite get over was the sense of responsibility that woman felt for being a boundary keeper for what she deemed appropriate and inappropriate in the house of God. I was later told several stories from sympathetic people who attended church regularly with her about the kind of chaos she created for her pastor and youth pastor as she consistently made herself the righteous judge of people's dress, behavior, and theology.

Certainly this woman represents an extreme, but nearly every day in the church and in Christian institutions, brokenness happens between brothers and sisters in Christ as judgments are made against one another. A pastor is forced to resign for speaking out against the war in Iraq. Drive-time radio is filled with messages regarding God's "righteous sentence" on areas torn apart by natural disaster. A congregation makes the prime-time news for becoming a human blockade at a local abortion clinic. A well-known academic society expels a handful of longtime members for not strictly adhering to a particular doctrinal tenet of the organization. The board of trustees votes to remove a seminary president supporting the ordination of women. A leading spokesperson for evangelicalism equates Christianity with one particular political party over another. The contract of a science professor at a Christian college is not renewed because she explores with her students the possibility of theistic evolution. A well-known and long-standing denomination is divided into multiple camps over the question of homosexuality.

The events above are meant to be hypothetical, yet most of us can recognize in our various Christian traditions moments when the pursuit of truth has turned into an angry, divisive, and hurtful dispute. Almost all of us are aware of moments when the ideological lines that form the boundaries of the church become the battlefronts for ugly interpersonal quarrels. The church in every era faces the continual challenge of warding off theological and philosophical attacks from within and without, while at the same time trying to maintain a posture of love and acceptance toward one another and the world—including our enemies.

A Culture of Change

Ephesus was a significant city economically, politically, and religiously. Located on four water passages, Ephesus was an important city for trade and culture. The population of Ephesus is estimated to have been between four hundred thousand and five hundred thousand at the time of John's writing, making it the largest city in Roman Asia and one of the largest cities of its day. The members of the church at Ephesus would have understood well the challenges of living out the faith in an urban context. Because of its size and significance, it is not surprising that John would begin his discourse to the seven churches with a letter to the church in Ephesus. "To the Christians . . . Ephesus stood for Asia, Asia was Ephesus."[1]

The church in Ephesus was birthed by Paul and left for a time under the care of Priscilla and Aquila. Later Paul would return to Ephesus for two and a half years to use the city as his home base. In Acts 19:23–41 we are told that Paul had to flee the city because of a dispute that began between the apostle and the artisans of the city whose livelihood depended on the sale of silver shrines of Artemis.

The temple built to the Greek goddess Artemis, who was known to the Romans as Diana, was central to the culture and religious atmosphere of Ephesus. Ephesus contained many of the great temples in Asia Minor, and the temple of Artemis was likely the pagan temple used the longest into the Christian era. The temple was 425 feet long, 220 feet in width, and 60 feet high.[2] Although we tend to think of the ancient temples and their idols as marble white in color, this temple was painted with bright colors and decorated with inlaid stone at the time it was in use. The statues of the gods or goddesses were painted to resemble enormous lifelike beings. Artemis was usually depicted either with many breasts or beside a deer and honored as the goddess of fertility, childbirth, and hunting.

Ephesus was one of the major centers for the emperor cult and the worship of the goddess Roma—the spiritual embodiment of the empire itself. One of the chief ways Rome honored its subject cities for their loyalty was to give the city permission and resources to build a temple to the emperors. Ephesus was bestowed this honor four times.[3]

Scholars often describe Ephesus as a city of change because it had a long history of political turmoil and because the very topography of the region was constantly in flux. Today, due to the continual buildup of silt in the harbor, the first-century port town of Ephesus sits five miles inland. As water turned to land, "the city followed the sea, and changed from place to place to maintain its importance as the only [harbor] of the valley."[4]

In a city filled with detestable pagan practices and powerful cultic ceremonies and shaken by the rapid changes of culture and landscape, how would the church survive? How would the Christians in Ephesus remain immovable in faith while standing on the literally shifting sands of their city? How would the Ephesian church stand for what was right in their constantly changing environment?

Boundary Keeping

The Revelator praises the Christians in Ephesus for their works, their toil, and their patient endurance (Rev. 2:2). Standing up against a pagan culture, false prophets, leadership instability, and the powerful lure of the empire, the Christians diligently worked and persevered by using what we might describe as strong filters for orthodoxy. Participation in a vibrant city of travel and commerce had to have meant that the church was continually confronted with itinerant teachers and philosophers claiming to be apostles and prophets. In the eyes of the Revelator, the Ephesian church had distinguished itself by "its insight into the true character of those who came to it with the appearance of Apostles. . . . But the Ephesian Church tested them all; and when they were false, unerringly detected them and unhesitatingly rejected them."[5] In his letter to the Ephesian church, the apostolic father and bishop, Ignatius, writes that the believers in Ephesus, "all live in accordance with the truth and that no heresy has found a home among [them]. Indeed, [they] do not so much as listen to anyone unless he speaks truthfully about Jesus Christ."[6]

In particular, John praises the church for their hatred of the works of the Nicolaitans (2:6). The nature of the Nicolaitan heresy, mentioned here and also in the letter to Pergamum (2:15), has been much debated. It appears that this sect lasted only a short time and primarily practiced a form of idolatry and immorality disguised as a deep spirituality. It is likely that the Nicolaitans made peace with the surrounding culture by participating in the cultic practices, such as eating meat sacrificed to idols and engaging in the sexual practices of the pagan temples.[7] It is possible that these forms of pagan practice were excused or even promoted by the Nicolaitans because they viewed these rituals as meaningless or empty, because the gods before whom these acts were committed were nothing. Or more deeply disturbing, the Nicolaitans might have viewed these pagan practices as deepening the spiritual sensitivity of those who participated in them.[8] Either way, John praises the Ephesian church for guarding its theological boundaries and recognizing that these practices are unacceptable for the Christian life.

Loss of Love

Yet in the midst of being praised for their persistence in keeping the faith, the Ephesian Christians are rebuked for abandoning "the love [they] had at first" (2:4). In their zeal for moral purity, they have lost the centrality of love. The question readers of this letter have to wrestle with is this: is there a connection between this church's hypersensitivity to moral purity and its lost first love? Is the Ephesian zeal for watching the boundaries of the community also the cause of their lost compassion? Can a community so focus on maintaining the orthodoxy of its theology that it loses its ability to love? Most commentators on Revelation seem to think that there is an important connection between the Ephesian church's heightened boundary keeping and the loss of their primary commission and passion: to make disciples of all peoples. As Robert Mounce writes, "Every virtue carries within itself the seeds of its own destruction. It seems probable that desire for sound teaching and the resulting forthright action taken to exclude all impostors had created a climate of suspicion in which love within the believing community could no longer exist."[9] Or as William Barclay states, "It may be that a hard, censorious, critical, fault-finding, stern self-righteousness had banished the spirit of love. . . . Strict orthodoxy can cost too much, if it has to be bought at the price of love."[10] Justo Gonzalez puts it this way: "Christians who are rightly concerned about the purity of faith and doctrine can become so obsessed by that concern that they begin looking at each other askance, and love is set aside. Orthodoxy becomes the hallmark of 'true faith,' and love seems to be of secondary importance."[11]

When John writes to the Ephesian church, "you have abandoned the love you had at first" (2:4), he is certainly including the love they have for God, but he seems to be emphasizing the love they were to continue to share with one another. Our love for God and our love for one another are deeply connected. Brokenness in our love for God inevitably leads to the shattering of our love for our neighbor. Love for others is the primary mark of Christian discipleship, but at Ephesus, hatred of heresy and closely guarding the boundaries of the faith had allowed the radiant light of love for God and one another to fade.

The result of a church becoming so preoccupied with defining doctrinal boundaries that they lose the divine spark of love that drew believers to faith in Christ is what Earl Palmer refers to as "The Ephesus Syndrome."[12] Few if any of us who are believers accepted Christ into our lives because we were doctrinally argued into the church. It was the love of God demonstrated in the life of the Spirit-filled body of Christ that wooed us into relationship with the Father. Unfortunately for the Ephesian church, in the pursuit of protecting its boundaries, it risked losing the very force that gave it life.

Ungenerous Orthodoxy

More than ever, today's church is confronted with the issues of rapid change. On the one hand, the pressures of an ever-changing culture mean that the church must constantly be vigilant to guard its life and keep its boundaries; but on the other hand, as the church has confronted change it has become a battlefield over worship, politics, and theology. Denominations, theological traditions, and local churches are constantly facing potential divisions over issues that range from minor to major. The deadly spirit of Ephesus that still has to be named and confronted is a spirit of boundary keeping. In the last century, the destructiveness of this first deadly spirit has been especially apparent in the deep splits both in historical denominations and in various Christian traditions such as liberalism, fundamentalism, evangelicalism, Pentecostalism, and the like.

The term "generous orthodoxy" was introduced by Hans Frei in an essay response to another theologian's critique of narrative theology.[13] Frei used the term to begin to describe his vision for a kind of theology that would move beyond what he believed was an outmoded dichotomy between traditions such as liberalism and fundamentalism.[14] *Generous orthodoxy* has more recently been used by philosophers, theologians, and church leaders such as Nancey Murphy, Stanley Grenz, and Brian McLaren as a way of describing an emerging theological sensibility that is trying to chart a path beyond the often-heated quarrels that have seemed to dominate the theological landscape between and within denominations and Christian traditions.[15]

Murphy is hopeful, from a philosophical perspective, that developing postmodern or "holist" approaches to epistemology will move traditions away from either/or theological perspectives that named people as in or out and will give a philosophical option to theologians seeking a middle way. As Murphy states, "My projection (and hope) is that theologians from both left and right will find resources in the new worldview for many fresh starts in theology. . . . And these new approaches ought to form more of a continuum or spectrum of theological options than a dichotomy."[16]

The late theologian Stanley Grenz also believes that "the time is ripe to reflect on the type of theological program that might result in a 'generous orthodoxy.'"[17] Like Murphy, Grenz thinks that the spirit that is both generous and orthodox will require more than just graciousness and civility on the part of liberal and conservative leaders; it will require a "renewed 'center' that lies beyond the polarizations of the past."[18] Grenz believes the potentially generous orthodox future of the church can be rediscovered as its people focus on the life-transforming power of the gospel, as they recognize that doctrinal formulas are always inadequate and somewhat transitory because they are constructed by particular churches within the linguistic, historical, and geographical particularity of their own contexts, and as the church becomes more catholic or more universal in scope.

Taking his cues in part from Murphy and Grenz, Brian McLaren writes to pastors and laypeople who have a concern for those outside the church. McLaren writes that as he experienced the deep divisions within the body of Christ, he often "felt like an ambulance driver bringing injured people to a hospital where there's an epidemic spreading among the patients and doctors and nurses."[19] McLaren's solution is not to abandon the idea that orthodoxy is right thinking but to link orthodoxy with orthopraxy (right living or the right practice of the gospel). As McLaren describes:

> Many orthodoxies have always and everywhere assumed that orthodoxy (right thinking and opinion about the gospel) and orthopraxy (right practice of the gospel) could and should be separated, so that one could at least be proud of getting an A in orthodoxy even when one earned a D in orthopraxy, which is only an elective class anyway. . . . In that traditional setting, orthodoxy could be articulated and debated by scholars or officials who had little responsibility to actually live by or live out the orthodoxy they defended. Defenders of orthodoxy were seen more like referees than basketball players; nobody cared if they could pass, dribble, or shoot, as long as they could blow a whistle and name an infraction in their black-and-white striped shirts. In contrast, . . . we are all on the court, so to speak. . . . You want to know the rules, not so you can blow whistles as a referee, but so you can have a lot of glorious good clean fun as a player, throwing passes and making assists and sinking three-pointers and layups without fouling out.[20]

Naming and confronting the spirit of boundary keeping and moving beyond the damaging disputes and ungenerous orthodoxy that have plagued the church throughout its history is not a call to dismiss doctrine as unimportant. As it was for the church in Ephesus, knowing what we believe and rightly believing it are critical any time, particularly in a culture of rapid change. However, there is something in this letter from the Revelator that desires the church in Ephesus to place orthopraxy (rightly living out the faith) or orthopathy (having the right heart or spirit) above orthodoxy (mentally assenting to correct doctrine as cognitive propositions).

As John the apostle makes famously clear in his first epistle, the demonstration that we are children of God is not that we believe the right set of propositions but that we embody the love of God in our relationships with one another. Those who know God love others, but those who do not know God do not love others. As John writes,

"No one has ever seen God; if we love one another, God lives in us, and his love is perfected in us" (1 John 4:12).

How does a church divided and broken by dogmatism and a spirit of boundary keeping recover the centrality of love? The Revelator begins by calling the Ephesian church to remember.

Remember

I was meeting not long ago with a married couple who were on the verge of divorce. The mutual animosity and resentment they had for each other had been allowed to grow for quite a while, and they were ready to call it quits. I was using all of my pastoral counseling training, but nothing was helping. It was clear that although they still coexisted in the same house, there was a tremendous amount of hostility between them.

Finally, in desperation I asked them to share with me where and how they fell in love. I had them share with me what attracted them to the other and what they had valued most about the other when they began dating. It was honestly not a counseling ploy; it was truly my desperate attempt to find out whether they ever really did like each other, but the question had an important effect. As they began to remember the love they originally had for each other and the feelings of genuine respect and care that had formed the basis of their relationship, they began to see and feel how far they had come from where they truly wanted to be with each other.

I have a professor friend who was forced to participate in what had the potential to be a very heated meeting between the religion faculty at a Christian university and a set of leaders from the university's sponsoring denomination. The denominational leaders were very upset with what some of them considered unorthodox theology being presented in several of the department's courses. All parties involved expected the meeting to be highly contentious. Knowing that everyone present was an ordained elder or minister in the church, the university administrator who was facilitating the meeting began by asking each professor and each denominational leader to tell the story of their call to ministry and to share their journey from divine call through ministerial preparation and ordination.

My friend recalls that from that point on, a potentially volatile meeting about strong differences of opinion became a gracious discussion set in a context of love. Why? Because remembering the common callings and sacrifices for the kingdom of both academics and pastors—the common bond of the love for Christ and his kingdom— allowed genuine theological differences to be discussed in an atmosphere of common grace.

The church in Ephesus is called to remember the earlier days in which the love of Christ abounded in the congregation. For the Revelator, remembering and restoring the centrality of love is not an option for the Christians at Ephesus. If love cannot triumph over their spirit of boundary keeping, Christ "will come to [them] and remove [their] lampstand from its place" (Rev. 2:5). This divine warning seems to mean that without the primacy of love Ephesus will be removed from the company of churches. In other words, when those who call themselves the church of Jesus Christ cease to have love for God, love for one another, and a passion for making disciples as its first priority and become a group of gatekeepers, that community ceases to be the church.

Unlike some of the denunciations that emerge in the following six letters, the ungenerous orthodoxy of the Ephesian church does not appear by the tone of this letter to be an irresolvable problem. The spirit of boundary keeping appears to be part of a natural struggle as the church tries to walk that fine line between nonconformity to the culture and obedience to the Spirit of Christ. If the church can recover its loving spirit, the Revelator writes, Christ will give them "permission to eat from the tree of life that is in the paradise of God" (2:7). In other words, the love and peace—*shalom*—that was originally lost to humankind in the garden because of rebellion against God and division between one another can be regained when the church learns how to fully love God and embrace one another.

There are many churches today that have produced in their life together an ugly spirit of ungenerous boundary keeping. It is natural that in a culture of rapid change our desire for purity and our fears of conformity would cause the church to fight for its boundaries. Unfortunately, being united by what we fear and what we hate is a poor substitute for being united in the love of Christ. "The commandment

we have from him is this: those who love God must love their brothers
and sisters also" (1 John 4:21).

Questions for Group Discussion

1. In what ways does the contemporary church engage in boundary keeping?
2. What happens to a church when boundary keeping becomes
   its primary purpose?
3. How can the church in the twenty-first century continue to hold
   tightly to the truth of the gospel without losing the centrality
   of Christian love?

2

Smyrna

The Spirit of Consumerism

"And to the angel of the church in Smyrna write: . . . I
know your affliction and your poverty, even though you
are rich. . . . Be faithful until death, and I will give you
the crown of life."

A recent article from the *New York Times* describes the construction of the new Swaminarayan Akshardham temple complex
in East Delhi as "the Disney Touch at a Hindu Temple."[1] This new
megatemple boasts "an indoor boat ride, a large-format movie screen,
a musical fountain and a hall of animatronic characters that may well
remind us that, really, it's a small world after all. There are even pink
(sandstone) elephants on parade."[2]

Obviously, the shocking aspect of this temple is that these unique
additions to a house of worship are being constructed by Hindus.
Western Christianity in recent years has become so accustomed to adding things borrowed from the secular culture—even from Disney—to

attract worshipers that such embellishments to an American mega-church would certainly not be of interest to the *Times* or any other national media organization. Perhaps the Hindus are learning something from Western religious culture. As the reporter states, "India already has a lot of Hindu temples, so if you want to persuade people to slip their shoes off for a new one, you've got to be imaginative."[3]

In North America, freedom of religion brings many blessings, including the freedom of religious choice. Unfortunately, the freedom to choose how to express one's spirituality has led to the commodification of the Christian faith. In many ways the gospel has become a product for sale by the church.

There are times when this commodification of the faith borders on the absurd. One can now purchase at select Christian bookstores and on the Internet such items as the Full Armor of God Pajamas, Holy Odor Eaters made from actual soil taken from Jerusalem, Mary or Jesus bobble-heads, a Pet Baptizing Kit complete with a certificate of baptism, Gospel Magic Glasses in which the face of Christ mysteriously appears when the glasses are filled with water, or (my personal favorite) the Holy Trinity Lego Set. Most of the commodification of the Christian faith, however, occurs in much more subtle ways. Pastors are trained in corporate models of church leadership. Churches adopt secular business strategies, such as branding, advertising, and market research, to compete with one another. It is no wonder that people looking to participate in a community of faith describe their search as "church shopping." People shop for a community of faith in the same way they shop for other products; they judge a church based on convenience, quality of ministry, personality fit, cost/benefit ratios, sermons that are relevant and easy to listen to, worship that fits their personal preferences and musical tastes, and so on.

Most recent studies across denominations show that although the number of Americans worshiping in a Christian church each Sunday has remained essentially flat over the last several decades, the number of megachurches that have been built during that same time period has exploded.[4] Although there are certainly many factors that have led to the rise of the megachurch, it is incontrovertible that the number of services (consumer services) large congregations are able to offer the church shopper is one of the major reasons these congregations continue to grow. In the market-driven culture of the West, we have let loose a powerful and potentially destructive spirit—the angel of consumerism.

A City of Suffering

The first-century city of Smyrna was an amazing city that had overcome a difficult history. Situated approximately thirty-five miles north of Ephesus, Smyrna was a prosperous port town. Of the seven cities addressed by the Revelator, Smyrna is the only one that continues as a thriving city—the Turkish city of Izmir.

Smyrna's location adjacent to a deep gulf made it highly desirable for nearly every major political power of the region for generations. Although it had been the site of many civil wars and conflicts, the city's prime location allowed it to be repeatedly rebuilt. Smyrna had been destroyed in 580 BCE by Alyattes, the king of neighboring Lydia, but was rebuilt in 290 BCE by Lysimachus and Antigonus as a model city. The rebuilt city of Smyrna boasted a famous stadium, a library, and the largest public theater in Asia.

Smyrna developed a special relationship with the rising superpower of Rome. From approximately 265 BCE to 146 BCE, while Rome was in a struggle for regional supremacy against the Carthaginian Empire, the citizens of Smyrna sided squarely with the Romans. Smyrna became the first city to build a temple to honor the goddess Roma (ca. 195 BCE) and later, in 23 BCE, was awarded the honor of building an additional temple to the emperor Tiberius. The city's ability to emerge from this nearly three-hundred-year period of abandonment (from destruction in 580 BCE to reestablishment in 290 BCE) and become one of the preeminent cities of the empire gave Smyrna the title, "The City That Died Yet Lives."[5] It should not surprise us, then, that the phrase used to describe the one who is speaking through the Revelator is the one "who was dead and came to life" (Rev. 2:8). Like the city of Smyrna, the one who judges the churches died, yet lives.

It was the popular practice of ancient historians and poets to associate the etymology of the name Smyrna with the valuable ancient resin *myrrh*. Although the two words sound similar, there is no evidence to support an etymological tie between the two words; "but there is evidence to support the belief that the coincidence was seen as significant in antiquity."[6] Given its history of political turmoil and frequent physical destruction, it is not surprising that in poetry and myth Smyrna became associated, like the valuable embalming ointment myrrh, with great suffering. But also like myrrh, the city became associated with the expectation of the overcoming of death through resurrection.

The credit for the resurrection of Smyrna belonged almost entirely to Rome. In the minds of the first-century citizens of Smyrna, it was because of their allegiance to Roma and to the gods of the empire that their life as a major city had been restored. In response to the blessings bestowed on it by Rome, Smyrna became a major site for emperor and cultic worship. The citizens of Smyrna wanted the city to continue to be a place where the gods would show favor to their faithful worshipers.

The majestic buildings that surrounded the city during the first century were especially symbolic of the gods' favor. As one approached the city by boat, the great buildings, including the acropolis on Mount Pagus, looked like a crown or garland adorning the cliffs, encouraging poets to speak of the spectacular skyline of the city as "the crown of Smyrna." The well-known majestic appearance of the reconstructed Smyrna may be behind the promise that those in the church who are "faithful until death" (2:10) will receive "the crown of life."[7]

A Church of Suffering

The church of Smyrna appears to have held a special place in John's heart. For John, there are two cities at work simultaneously in Smyrna. On the one hand, the city itself had endured great suffering, but in giving itself over to the empire of Rome it has received its reward—a crown of buildings, wealth, and honor. On the other hand, the second city in Smyrna, the church, like its host city, is now facing a period of struggle and a time of possible death.

The church in Smyrna faced threats from two directions. The first threat came from the empire of Rome itself. Rome continually faced

the problem of how to unify an empire that covered such a vast terri-
tory and included so many different cultures, languages, and histories.
Something was required to unite all of the diverse citizens of Rome into
a unified collective. As Barclay writes, "None of the extant religions
was capable of being universalized. But one thing was capable of being
universalized—the spirit of Rome itself."[8] The peace that had been
established by Rome—the *Pax Romana*—had made life easier, orderly,
and prosperous. "It was not difficult to turn the spirit of Rome into a
power which men were gratefully willing to worship."[9]

It became a practice of the ensuing emperor worship that once a
year a citizen was required to burn a pinch of incense on the altar to
caesar. Having done so, citizens were given a certificate that verified
they had participated in their civic duty. Although participation in
this kind of ceremony had religious overtones, it was primarily a
political statement. Those who refused to participate would be held
in both religious contempt and political suspicion. Imagine being at
a professional sporting event and the person sitting next to you not
only refusing to stand and remove their hat during the singing of the
national anthem but also turning away from the flag and with their
body language making it clear to all around them that they were not
going to give attention, let alone honor, to the flag. How would that
person be viewed and treated by those who witnessed their lack of
participation? Even in a democratic society like America where the
freedoms of speech and of public demonstration are protected, a
person who openly defies a moment of patriotism risks social stig-
matization and bodily injury.

If a person in modern-day America is held in suspicion for not
participating in a routine act of allegiance to the state, how much
more would a first-century city like Smyrna, where Rome was highly
treasured as the great benefactor in the city's rebirth, hold in suspicion those who refused to participate in the ceremonies of emperor
worship? Like the fate of the Hebrew children who refused to bow
to Nebuchadnezzar's idol, the believers of Smyrna faced the persis-
tent threat of political persecution from an empire that held them in
suspicion.

A second and more challenging hazard came from the community
of Jews living in the city. The people of Smyrna had espoused the

ideals of Rome and were granted several privileges because of their allegiance to the empire. Because of this, Smyrna had a very open citizenship policy. This openness made the city one of the major population centers for Judaism and an area in which Jews were granted comparatively significant political rights. For example, Jews could worship their God freely as long as they were willing to participate in various civic aspects of the city's life.

The Revelator writes that the Lord of the church knows "the slander on the part of those who say that they are Jews and are not, but are a synagogue of Satan" (2:9). Although we must be careful not to use this statement to justify anti-Semitism—certainly the acts of persecution that were done to the Christians by the Jews in Smyrna pale in comparison to the horrible acts of persecution that Christians have engaged in against Jews throughout history—it is nevertheless clear that great conflict arose between the church in Smyrna and some of the city's Jewish citizens. It is likely that the Jews of Smyrna were given an exemption from participating in the cultic practices of emperor worship. As long as they did not stir up trouble in the city, they were not conscripted into the imperial cult but were allowed to worship Yahweh freely.

Although many of the Christians in Smyrna were certainly Jewish, gentiles were also converting to the Christian faith. It is probable that the gentile believers responded to their faith by no longer participating in the cultic worship practices of the empire and claiming exemption from those rites based on the fact that they now belonged to a Jewish faith. In the eyes of the empire, however, these new believers were not Jews; they were gentiles. From the perspective of the Jews of Smyrna, these believers were seen as a threat to their peaceable way of life because whatever political waves they created with the Roman leaders carried the potential of wiping out the civic privileges granted to the Jewish citizens. So, although the new believers claimed to be part of a Jewish faith, they were openly rejected by the Jewish citizens of Smyrna, leaving them outside the umbrella of protection afforded the Jewish population and thus vulnerable to persecution.

John also acknowledges in his letter that he is aware of their poverty (2:9). It is likely that this poverty is a literal material poverty and not poverty in a spiritual sense. The economic welfare of the believers of

Smyrna was certainly threatened because of their faith. As George Eldon Ladd states, "We may assume that the poverty of the Smyrneans was not due alone to their normal economic condition but to confiscation of property, looting by hostile mobs, and to the difficulty of earning a living in a hostile environment."[10]

In addition to economic threats, the church in Smyrna was faced with the threat of death. The Revelator writes: "Beware, the devil is about to throw some of you into prison so that you may be tested, and for ten days you will have affliction. Be faithful until death, and I will give you the crown of life" (2:10). It seems unlikely that "ten days" is meant to symbolize a short period of time. If the Revelator followed his usual pattern, he would use the number forty, which is the symbolic number for a short period of time that eventually ends. It is more likely that ten days is the average period of time between being taken into custody by the state, being tried for treason, and being publicly executed.[11] The Roman state did not like to burden itself with long incarceration periods for criminals; thus prisoners usually faced fines, exile, or immediate death. It seems clear that John believes many of the Christians in Smyrna would face death, being spurned by the Jewish population and executed by the Roman authorities.

The Rich Poor

Although the church faced difficult persecution, there is almost a subversive nature in the way the Revelator views the status of the church in Smyrna in contrast to the city itself. From the perspective of earth, the *city* of Smyrna is rich and powerful. The city wears the crown bestowed on it by the empire. From the perspective of earth, the *Christians* of Smyrna are not only poor and foolish but also suspicious outsiders who refuse to participate in the systems of power that make the city great.

From the perspective of heaven, however, the *city* of Smyrna is poor because it has placed its hope and trust in powers that cannot survive "the second death" (2:11). The "crown of Smyrna," which was the city's source of pride, will eventually crumble into ruin like all material objects. From the perspective of heaven, the *church* of Smyrna is rich because its members have oriented their life together toward a crown of life that never fades and can never be taken away.

It is interesting given the great pressures the church in Smyrna faced during the first century that of the seven churches only the church of Smyrna still exists. Smyrna, now Izmir, remains a vibrant center of Eastern Orthodox worship and education. The practice of Christian faith has never been easy in Smyrna. There have been various forms of political pressure and persecution over the last nineteen centuries, but its faith still speaks.[12]

It is difficult for us to hear this text today because we are comparatively so wealthy and we have so many freedoms. In many places in North America it is beneficial politically, socially, and often financially to claim the Christian faith as one's own. How do we hear this word to the suffering church in Smyrna in a nonoppressive and nonpersecuting society? Despite its lack of power and prosperity, there was something about the church in Smyrna that caused Jesus, through John, to express profound passion. The Lord of the churches assessed Smyrna as a great church. Although we are in obviously different historical contexts, is there something the North American church can learn from the spirit of the Smyrnaean church about what Christ desires his church to be?

It is important as pastors and lay leaders in the church that we ask the following question: "What does a good church look like?" When I was a professor, this was the single question that we gave to students as a final evaluation of their years of undergraduate theology and ministry study. I have read hundreds of student essays attempting to answer this question. I could evaluate those papers as a professor because back then I was pretty sure I knew the answer to that question. But then I became a pastor. Now I realize I have less certainty than I thought about what a good church looks like and even less idea how to lead one into existence.

In a culture of complete freedom, like ours, people tend to believe that a good church is one that gives a great deal but requires very little of its members. In 1985, sociologist Robert Bellah and his team of researchers published a critically praised and highly influential study on American life titled *Habits of the Heart: Individualism and Commitment in American Life*. In their study, Bellah and his team tried to answer the following question: in a culture that is founded in and profoundly shaped by the ideals of individualism, why do Americans make commitments and how are those commitments sustained? Their study led them to conclude that Americans have four ways of speaking—or possess four vocabularies—when they talk about their commitments. Those four ways of speaking can be described as two vocabularies of individualism (utilitarian and expressive) and two vocabularies of commitment (citizenship and covenant).[13] The vocabulary of utilitarian individualism essentially asks the following questions about making commitments: What is in it for me? If I make this commitment, what will I receive in return that will benefit my life? Do the utilitarian benefits of this commitment outweigh the costs? Expressive individualism is also a vocabulary focused on self, but rather than asking what utilitarian benefits can be gained, it is a way of speaking about commitment that focuses on the emotional or therapeutic benefits of a commitment. Expressive individualism asks: If I make this commitment, how will I feel? Will I feel better because I have placed myself in this relationship?

For Bellah, individualism, in either its utilitarian or its expressive forms, "is the first language in which Americans tend to think about their lives."[14] The problem of individualism being the first language of a people, however, is that relationships become very difficult to sustain. Bellah gives examples of interview subjects who describe their commitment to a spouse using only the vocabularies of utilitarian and expressive individualism. A husband expresses his commitment to his wife in terms of everything she does for him, or a wife explains her commitment to her husband in terms of all of the ways he makes her feel. But what happens, Bellah's team of sociologists wonders, if and when she can no longer do all those things for him or he can no longer make her feel what she currently feels? What vocabulary will exist in the American consciousness for sustaining that relationship? The danger of a culture that is immersed almost exclusively in vocabularies of individualism is that "individualism has been sustainable in the United States only because it has been supported and checked by other, more generous moral understandings."[15] In other words, a culture that is established on the rights of the individual is helpful and beneficial as long as that culture is tempered by other coexisting worldviews that contain vocabularies that give coherence to commitments beyond the rugged individual. But what happens to relationships in a culture of individualism when those other counterbalancing vocabularies of community and commitment cease to exist?

Bellah and his team discovered that the Americans they studied said they would remain in their primary commitments even if the individualistic reasons for being in the commitment were gone, but they either did not have or only possessed remnants of the "more generous" vocabularies that provided the bases for staying in those relationships of commitment. In other words, Bellah and his team discovered that the American husband who loves his wife because of what she does and the American wife who loves her husband for how he makes her feel would stay with that spouse even if they can no longer provide those utilitarian or expressive benefits. But Bellah (et al.) also discovered that most Americans have lost the vocabulary to describe *why* they would stay with a commitment in which the individualistic value is gone. Americans, according to Bellah, have the habits of the heart for sustaining commitment but they have lost (or are rapidly losing) the vocabularies that make those commitments coherent.

Bellah found two groups of people who were exceptions to the dominant utilitarian and expressive individualists. The two segments of the population who retained a coherent language of commitment speak vocabularies of citizenship and/or covenant. The language of citizenship is a language "guided by the nation's founders . . . which places upon citizens a responsibility for the welfare of their fellows and for the common good."[16] A covenant (or biblical) tradition teaches "concern for the intrinsic value of individuals because of their relationship to the transcendent. It asserts the obligation to respect and acknowledge the dignity of all."[17] Both the citizenship and the covenant traditions are juxtaposed to the vocabularies of individualism in the ways they affirm the social dimension of human persons. In other words, Bellah argues that over the long term, habits of the heart are not enough to sustain the commitments necessary for community. Healthy societies must also maintain a vocabulary that gives to its citizens a logic for remaining committed beyond the pursuits of individualism.

It is apparent to Bellah that the vocabulary of citizenship is being increasingly undermined by a culture of individualism. The republican vocabulary of citizenship was employed by those who came to America with strong ethnic ties, who lived through the hardships of the Great Depression, and who experienced the strong national bond that arose out of the World Wars. During the era of the two World Wars, the military could recruit simply by having the image of Uncle Sam proclaim "I Need You." Today, the army must promise recruits that joining its ranks will help them to "Be All You Can Be." The army's change in method is an example of citizenship in an age that has lost the vocabulary of citizenship.

What Bellah believes is needed in a nation struggling through the effects of the rising dominance of vocabularies of individualism is the counterbalancing influence of communities of memory. Communities of memory are real communities of people who do not forget their past. They do so by being "involved in retelling its story, its constitutive narrative, and in so doing, it offers examples of the men and women who have embodied and exemplified the meaning of the community."[18] These communities of memory speak, model, and embody the life of covenant. The best communities for keeping this memory alive, according to Bellah, are churches, synagogues, and other locations of worship.[19]

It seems to me that even the casual observer of American life can easily see the changing effects the vocabularies of individualism are having on the social fabric of the culture. However, the casual observer of the religious culture in America also notices that just when the culture needs the church to be speaking its native vocabulary of covenant, it too is abandoning this vocabulary and replacing it with those of utilitarian and expressive individualism. In American pulpits, Jesus is routinely offered as the antidote for failing businesses, failing finances, and failing relationships. Although I deeply believe that there is not only wisdom but also miraculous transformative power in relationship with Christ, I am convinced that what is often said (and what is most often heard) is the offer of a Messiah who can give us the desire of our utilitarian, individualistic hearts. Even if we shy away from a health-and-wealth gospel shaped by utilitarian pursuits, we often offer a therapeutic Jesus who is the cure for our feelings of loneliness, inadequacy, and purposelessness connected to the vocabulary of expressive individualism. Again, although I do believe there is a resource of joy to be found in relationship with Christ that cannot be found in any other source, the transformative work of God in Christ goes beyond therapeutic patterns.

Bellah summarizes:

> We thus face a profound impasse. Modern individualism seems to be producing a way of life that is neither individually nor socially viable, yet a return to traditional forms would be to return to intolerable discrimination and oppression. The question, then, is whether the older civic and biblical traditions have the capacity to reformulate themselves while simultaneously remaining faithful to their own deepest insights.[20]

Whether they recognize it or not, all preachers face the temptation to shape the gospel—which calls disciples to leave everything behind and take up their cross daily and follow Jesus, committing themselves as a needed part in the body of Christ—into a commodity that will be attractive to a culture conversant in the vocabularies of individualism. So instead of calling people to count the cost of discipleship, we create specialized ministries and build churches that look like malls, coffee shops, and pizza places. Reaching people where they are is necessary, but too often we reinforce individualism by making the church solely a place where individuals are fed but where not much is expected from anyone.

Returning to the church of Smyrna, it appears Jesus praises this church because the Christians there were willing to risk so much. The Jewish synagogue, fearful of losing its privileges, became not a place to worship God but a "synagogue of Satan." The true church that receives blessing from the mouth of Jesus is the church that is able to give so little to its members while requiring so much. The believers there had so little to gain, but they risked so much.

Polycarp

The oldest written account of a Christian martyrdom outside the New Testament is the death of Polycarp, the bishop of Smyrna, who was burned at the stake around 156 CE. Tradition tells us that Polycarp may have been one of John's disciples. The account of Polycarp's death sheds light on the threats facing the early church. "The Martyrdom of Polycarp sets out quite clearly both the issue at stake—Lord Christ versus Lord Caesar—and the state's (as well as the general population's) view of Christians as disloyal atheists who threatened the well-being of the empire."[21] Here is part of the moving account of Polycarp's death:

> The whole multitude, marveling at the bravery of the God-loving and God-fearing race of Christians, began shouting, "Away with the atheists! Find Polycarp!" . . .
> Polycarp entered the stadium. . . . The proconsul tried to persuade him to recant, saying, "Have respect for your age," and other such things as they are accustomed to say: "Swear by the genius of Caesar; repent; say, 'Away with the atheists!'" So Polycarp solemnly looked at the whole crowd of lawless heathen who were in the stadium, motioned toward them with his hand, and then (groaning as he looked up to heaven) said, "Away with the atheists!" . . .
> But when the magistrate persisted and said, "Swear the oath, and I will release you; revile Christ," Polycarp replied, "For eighty-six years I have been his servant, and he has done me no wrong. How can I blaspheme my King who saved me?" . . .
> "I am a Christian."[22]

Polycarp was then burned at the stake for his faith. He prayed a prayer before the fire was lit that he would become an acceptable sacrifice for Christ. When the fire was lit, the account of his martyrdom states that the aroma of his death was "like bread baking or like gold and silver being refined in a furnace."[23] In standing up for Christ, Polycarp became the embodiment of the living bread. I am humbled by the Christians in Smyrna because in so many ways it is too easy for us to be Christian today. In a culture as prosperous as Smyrna, and America, it is a constant temptation to believe that a good church is one that gives much but requires very little.

This letter is particularly troubling for me as the pastor of a large metropolitan church. It is too easy for a church like mine to define being a "good church" by pointing to all the ways we are able to cater to the church shopper. In a culture steeped in the vocabulary of consumption, how do we become the church that gives much but requires even more? The holy life that brings honor to God is the life where much is given but much is also required.

Questions for Group Discussion

1. In what ways has the modern church turned the gospel into a commodity?
2. How can the church meet people's spiritual needs without turning them into "church shoppers"?
3. What role can the church play in shaping the vocabulary of its members away from utilitarian and expressive individualism and toward a vocabulary of covenant with God and with one another?

3

Pergamum

The Spirit of Accommodation

> "And to the angel of the church in Pergamum write: . . .
> I know where you are living, where Satan's throne is. Yet
> you are holding fast to my name . . . even in the days of
> Antipas my witness. . . . But I have a few things against
> you: you have some there who hold to the teaching of
> Balaam."

The people of God have always found themselves confronted by an empire. In the biblical narratives, empires such as Egypt, Canaan, Assyria, Babylon, Persia, and Rome in various ways and at various times confronted and challenged the ability of God's people to remain faithful witnesses to his lordship in the world. It has become the practice of some biblical interpreters to merge these various principalities and powers into one collective whole termed "empire."[1] *Empire* is the name given to the spiritual or social nature of a nation, culture, or political entity that overtly and covertly pervades every area of the lives of those living within it, conforming those persons to the shared values, identities, and convictions of the ruling powers. Like the angels of the churches, empires (or principalities and powers) can be agents for good or evil, but their tendency to make their power and existence ultimate is subversive to the kingdom of God.

When the apostle Paul exhorts the early church to "not be conformed to this world, but be transformed by the renewing of your minds" (Rom. 12:2), he is referring to the work of "empire" in shaping us into its image and to the Hebraic understanding of the nature of humankind itself. The creation narratives of Genesis tell us that humankind is created in God's image (Gen. 1:26–27). One of the most important aspects of this assertion for ancient Israel was the idea that humankind is uniquely created to be God's image or reflection in the world. In the creation narratives, Adam and Eve are created to be reflections of God's loving character to each other, to the rest of creation, and even, in some sense, to themselves. Each day that they walked in unbroken relationship with God they also lived in harmony with each other and creation. They were able to be naked and vulnerable with the world because of their proper sense of self-love. Once sin entered the picture because of human disobedience, the severed relationship with God led to blame between our first parents, brokenness in their proper dominion of creation, and even shame and the need to hide their life from God and from each other.

Nevertheless, although the image of God in humankind was marred, Israel still believed that human beings are uniquely formed by God to be reflections of him to the world. This is at least part of the reason why the second of the Ten Commandments expressly forbids the fashioning of images. God does not forbid material representations of himself simply because he is too vast to be fairly represented or because (like most of us) he has "image issues." I have never seen a picture of me that I have liked. Every time I see a picture of myself I think, "My nose isn't that crooked is it?" Or, "Does my hair really stick up like that in the back?" God's problem is not that we don't have craftsmen skilled enough to create a fair likeness of him. The problem is that he has already created an image of himself: humankind. We human beings are created to be his image in the world.

The tension between being God's image, or more properly his imagers, on the one hand, and being pushed, pulled, and shaped by the empire, on the other hand, is clearly seen in the story of the exodus. Not only is the basic plot of the exodus event the primary story for the Old Testament, but it is also perhaps the basic plotline for the entire story of God's redemption. God hears the cries of broken and enslaved people, is moved by their pleas for mercy, and moves to bring about salvation, transformation, and freedom.

In the midst of God's redemption of Israel, a kind of cosmic battle takes place between God and the embodiment of the oppressive empire, Pharaoh. It is interesting that at the beginning of the exodus narratives Scripture tells us the names of two culturally insignificant Hebrew midwives, Shiphrah and Puah (who nevertheless become significant instruments of salvation), but never reveals the name of Pharaoh, the most significant political and cultural leader of the day. By excluding the Pharaoh's particular name, the author may be initiating the reader into the subversive economy of God, an economy that considers the first to be last and the last to be first. It may also be that Pharaoh's name is not included because, for the writers of Scripture, every Pharaoh is the same. Every Pharaoh inevitably embodies the oppressive values of the empire and exploits, oppresses, and enslaves others.

So the political questions of the exodus are these: Who is the real god/God—the visible Pharaoh or the invisible Yahweh? Who really controls creation—the dominating empire or the loving creator? Who really has the final word over the issues of life and death—Pharaoh the conquering warlord or Yahweh the merciful peacemaker? Who has the authority to determine the lives of others—the gods of the rich and mighty or the God of the enslaved? And most importantly, with whom will the people side and find their ultimate identity—the king of Egypt or the God of Moses?

In the last of the ten plagues, the children of Israel are asked to decide with which power, Pharaoh or Yahweh, they are willing to literally mark their lives: "Your lamb shall be without blemish. . . . [You] shall take some of the blood and put it on the two doorposts and the lintel of the houses in which [you] eat it. . . . The blood shall be a sign for you on the houses where you live: when I see the blood,

I will pass over you, and no plague shall destroy you when I strike the land of Egypt" (Exod. 12:5, 7, 13).

On that Passover night the question is, will the people place their trust in the power of the visible empire of Pharaoh that surrounds them and has been the taskmaster of their lives, or will they put their hope and faith in the God represented by the weakness and vulnerability of the slain lamb? Those who marked their lives and their homes with the lamb are redeemed. Yet even after leaving their bondage to Pharaoh, the people are still confronted in the wilderness and in the land of Canaan by all the foreign nations with their false gods and pagan practices. As the redeemed children of God, the people are to make sure that they continually mark their lives with the singular worship of God. In one of the most important texts from the Mosaic Law, a text often referred to by the Hebrew word that opens it—the Shema—the people receive the following command: "Hear, O Israel: The LORD is our God, the LORD alone. You shall love the LORD your God with all your heart, and with all your soul, and with all your might. Keep these words that I am commanding you today in your heart. . . . Bind them as a sign on your hand, fix them as an emblem on your forehead, and write them on the doorposts of your house and on your gates" (Deut. 6:4–9).

The key idea in the Shema is that the people again mark their lives, in ways not unlike the marking of Passover, with faithful worship of God. Unfortunately, the values and convictions of the surrounding nations rubbed off on the Israelites, and they eventually demanded from Samuel and from God a king so that they could be "like all the other nations" (1 Sam. 8:20 NIV). They received their king, but just as God had warned, the people ended up in exile again. This time they were exiled to the nation of Babylon. Unlike the oppressive rule of Egypt, the danger in Babylon was that the people, and the Hebrew children in particular, would be lured into the practices and values of this foreign empire. In the early narratives of the book of Daniel, we find that the best and brightest of the Hebrew children were tempted to sit at King Nebuchadnezzar's table, bow to his authority, and in so doing lose their distinctive identity, their constitutive practices, and their unique way of life.

Although God did redeem the children of Israel from Babylon, when the New Testament opens we find the people again subject to a dominating empire. The ministry of Jesus and the kingdom he established were continually confronted by the challenge of Rome. The people Jesus lived among and ministered to wrestled daily with the question, how do we live as resident aliens and citizens of God's kingdom in a culture that runs counter to the values of God's reign?

Once, when asked by the temple lawyers whether it was lawful to pay taxes to caesar, Jesus took a denarius and asked this important question: whose image is on this coin (see Mark 12:16)? In turning the question back on the religious leaders, Jesus essentially tells the crowd to give back to caesar everything that bears the image of the empire but to give back to God everything that bears the divine image. What bears the divine image? Humankind bears the image of God. It should not surprise us, then, that the epistles to the early church call followers of Jesus to not conform to the world—to the image of the empire that surrounds us—but to be conformed to the image of Christ, who "is the image of the invisible God" (Col. 1:15). How is the church to live in the world but not be of it?

Pergamum: The Image of Empire

Pergamum was not as important a commercial city as Ephesus or Smyrna, but it was more important as a political and religious center. Because it did not have the economic benefits of other cities, the citizens decided that its life would be most blessed by orienting the city toward bringing glory to the empire. The leaders in Pergamum knew that their city could never match the splendor of Rome, but it could try to become the reflection—the image—of Rome on the eastern side of the empire. The hope was that when people came to Pergamum they would know that there was a powerful empire in the world because that empire's life would be reflected in the life of the city. As a way of honoring the empire, Pergamum became one of the major seats for emperor worship.

These are the words of him who has the sharp two-edged sword . . . (Rev. 2:12).

Pergamum was granted the authority to be the judgment seat of the east, so in essence the city bore the sword for Rome. In honor of the emperor Diocletian, the citizens built an arena where gladiatorial games could take place. Huge feasts and festivals were held for those in authority. Graphic and violent displays were staged as a way of celebrating the power and might of Rome. Criminals of various kinds would have their hands cut off and then be thrown into the arena with wild beasts. Cheered on by the mobs in attendance, the Romans toiled to find more creative ways to celebrate violence. The justification for such cruelty was that punishment was being enacted on criminals.

Of the seven Asian cities addressed by the Revelator, Pergamum was the one in which a faithful church was most likely to clash with the surrounding culture, which was immersed in the imperial cult. In this provincial capital, which was granted the power to execute people at will, the sovereign Christ with the two-edged sword reminds the oppressed and threatened church that ultimate power over life and death belongs only to God.

I know where you are living, where Satan's throne is (Rev. 2:13).

Although some scholars think this may be an allusion to the worship of the god Asclepius, the serpent god of healing, it is more likely that John is referring to Pergamum as the location of Satan's throne because of the lethal combination of emperor worship and pagan practice that defined the city. Pergamum was the first city in Asia to openly support the imperial cult. In fact, in 29 BCE a temple was dedicated "to the divine Augustus and the goddess Roma."[2] In addition to its practice of the imperial cult, the city also had an acropolis (a high city or "sacred rock") that sat almost one thousand feet above the surrounding land, on which had been erected several temples to a variety of pagan deities, such as Zeus, Athena, and Asclepius.

The Church of Pergamum: Failed Witness

The question the Christians of Pergamum faced was that of witness. To what divine power were they going to bear witness? Were they going to witness, like the city itself, to Rome, or were they going to image the life of the Creator of the universe and the Father of Jesus Christ?

The letter to the church references the teaching of Balaam (2:14), who in the book of Numbers (Num. 22–24) became the biblical

prototype of a corrupt teacher who led believers into fatal compromise with the daughters of Moab. Apparently at Pergamum,
some within the church were teaching that accommodation with
the culture was the wisest political policy. If the sin of Ephesus was
harsh intolerance, the sin of the church at Pergamum was spiritual
laxity and tolerance without spiritual discernment.

It would be difficult to understand the prohibition in the letter
against meat sacrificed to idols (Rev. 2:14) as a restriction against
buying meat sold in the open market. Paul had dealt with that issue
already in 1 Corinthians 7–8.[3] Therefore, it seems likely that the Revelator is referring to the active participation of Christians in the temple
feasts meant to honor the pagan deities. These feasts were filled with
ceremonies to honor the gods or the emperor and were packed with
rich food and strong drink that usually led to orgy-like celebrations
that overflowed with every form of debauchery. Sexual laxity was not
considered a serious sin by the ancient Greeks and Romans. But for
John, to give one's body to the practices of the empire in this way
was to mark or identify one's life with the empire rather than to be
marked with or formed by the life of the Lamb of God. Although
the church at Pergamum claimed Christ as Lord, they were accom-
modating themselves to the primary social, economic, and political
practices of the surrounding culture. In so doing, they were failing
to reflect the character of Christ properly and were being shaped and
conformed into the image of the dominant culture.

A Faithful Witness

John refers to a faithful witness to Christ, Antipas (Rev. 2:13), who
was almost certainly one of the earliest martyrs in Pergamum. Some
scholars have speculated that the unusual name Antipas may have
originally been given to this person in honor of Herod Antipas, the son
of Herod the Great who ruled over Galilee during the time of Christ's
ministry. It may be the case, therefore, that Antipas the martyr was a
radical convert from allegiance to Rome to commitment to Christ.

Biblical scholar Bruce Longenecker has written a fascinating novel
based on the character of Antipas titled *The Lost Letters of Per-*

gamum.[4] In this very creative work, Longenecker writes a series of letters between Antipas and the author of the third gospel, Luke. Longenecker works from the assumption that Antipas was a dedicated Pergamum citizen who was leading the way in the building of a library and scheduling great arena events in honor of the empire. He writes Luke to ask him to send any books he can from the library of Theophilus (the person to whom Luke addresses both the Gospel of Luke and the Book of Acts) for this new library. Luke agrees to send some of Theophilus's books, but he includes in the shipment the Gospel he has written and asks for Antipas to read it and give him his review and reaction to it. As Antipas reads the story of Jesus, he and Luke correspond about it.

The more Antipas reads about the life of Christ, the more questions he has. Luke encourages him to meet with a household of Christians who would also like to read Luke's Gospel and who might also be able to help answer his questions. In one such house group, Antipas discovers a wealthy group of "believers" who have a keen interest in Jesus but who live as normal citizens of the city, participating in all its cultic practices. As he reads from the Gospel of Luke, this group is confronted with the teaching of Jesus regarding the dangers of wealth and the need to give up one's life for the sake of the kingdom. The people snicker at these ideas and dismiss Jesus as an idealist. They love the miracle stories and are deeply attracted to Jesus's displays of power, but they see his call to serve others as simply the moral ravings of a peasant.

Antipas attends another house meeting at which he discovers a very different and somewhat disconcerting setting. Not only are the poor and crippled present in this upper-class home, but the master of the house, Antonius, serves everyone himself. Although Antonius was wealthy and a person of great significance, he washes the feet of the guests as they enter his home. Upon entering the house, Antipas is handed a basket of bread by the master of the house and is invited to help him serve those who are present. This culturally improper reversal of roles makes Antipas extremely uncomfortable.

Also in attendance at the house meeting is a man named Simon, a former servant in Antipas's home. Having released him from his service because of his age, Antipas anticipated that Simon would have died of hunger. So Antipas is shocked to discover that Antonius has saved

Simon by bringing him into his home as a bookkeeper. In the unique community present in the house of Antonius, not only do Antipas and Simon—former master and former slave—eat together at the same table, but Antipas is also asked to serve the very one he used and discarded.

The atmosphere of service is very difficult for Antipas to endure, yet something about the unique love and Christlikeness of the home of Antonius draws him in. Antipas eventually responds in faith to the love of Christ that he experiences through Antonius and the other believers there. The story is too long to fully recount here, suffice it to say that by the time the next arena games are held in Pergamum, Antonius's household church has come under suspicion for subversive Christian practice. Before one of Antipas's new brothers and sisters in Christ is killed in the arena, Antipas stands up from among the people and witnesses before the emperor that "no one is more surprised than I am to find that what motivates me now is not a commitment to the *Pax Romana* [the peace brought about by Rome] but a commitment to the empire of the God of Israel. . . . Should Rome's justice require a victim, then let that victim be me. I will take his punishment."[5] Caesar permits the substitution, and Antipas is placed inside the carcass of a bull and roasted alive.

Two Powers

What I find so fascinating about Longenecker's enlightened imagination about Antipas is both the way Antipas became a witness in the arena and the way in which the genuine Christian community he discovered in Antonius's home also served as a counterwitness to the life of the empire. John recognizes in this letter that the empire carries the power to coerce people to do its bidding because it bears the sword of death, but the power of Christ is far superior because Christ alone bears the double-edged sword of truth that divides false power from divine power (2:12; see also Heb. 4:12). The empire has the power to make war on its enemies (Rev. 2:16), but Christ is Lord over the principalities and powers by winning a "holy war" using the truth of his Word. The methodology of the "holy war" of the Lamb stands in sharp contrast to the warring methodologies of the empire. The war of the Lamb is articulated by Paul: "Do not repay anyone

evil for evil, but take thought for what is noble in the sight of all. . . .
If your enemies are hungry, feed them; if they are thirsty, give them
something to drink. . . . Do not be overcome by evil, but overcome
evil with good" (Rom. 12:17, 20–21). The empire conquers its enemies
through death (Rev. 2:13), but the Spirit and love of Christ ultimately
conquer evil with good. The empire can threaten with exile and hunger
those who do not conform, but Christ offers manna (2:17), sustenance
that the world does not comprehend. The empire can exclude those
who do not profess their allegiance to its power, but Christ offers to
the faithful the white stone (2:17), or tessera—most likely the ancient
equivalent of a ticket of admission—as a token of eternal acceptance
to and inclusion in his divine banquet. What Antipas responds to and
accepts is the way of the Lamb reflected in the Pergamum church, and
in his embrace of the community of Christ, the image of the beast—
the true character of the Roman Empire—is revealed.

The Mark of the Beast

There are several images that John gives in Revelation to encourage
the first-century Christians as they refuse to accommodate their lives
to the dominant culture and live as witnesses to the kingdom of God.
In Revelation 13, John gives three images that speak profoundly to the
struggle that, like the Christians of Pergamum, we too find ourselves
in. The first is a beast that rises out of the sea and gives the empire its
great coercive power (13:1–10). Many biblical scholars assert that this
beast is a symbol of Rome's military power that gives it "authority
over every tribe and people and language and nation" (13:7).

The second beast rises from the earth and lures the world into
worshiping the empire (13:11–18). In many ways, this second beast is
more insidious and dangerous than the first because it "had two horns
like a lamb and it spoke like a dragon" (13:11). In other words, this
second beast, which scholars point to as a symbol of the imperial cult
and the religious atmosphere of the empire, can often look like the
right thing—it looks like the Lamb—but in its heart and at its core it
still speaks like the empire. This image reminds me of the first home
Antipas visits in Longenecker's book. Those who desire the power that

Jesus possesses but who do not want to become his followers in love and service too often look like the Lamb but are in reality denizens of empire. When one reads the thirteenth chapter of Revelation, one gets the sense that John realizes that the military and violent threat the empire wields is certainly dangerous to the church. But even more dangerous to the thriving of the kingdom of God are people like the accommodated believers of Pergamum, who have placed Jesus on the shelf with all the other gods of the culture and have turned the church into a reflection of the beast rather than of the Lamb.

Also in the thirteenth chapter of Revelation we get the well-known image of the mark of the beast, placed on the right hand or forehead, with its number of six hundred sixty-six (13:16–18). Certainly there has been plenty of speculation regarding the mark of the beast over the last century. Unlike some popular apocalyptic writers, I am convinced that the mark is not a microchip, bar code, or tattoo that will some day be forced on those who wish to buy or sell in the world's economy; rather, it is a theological symbol that has its roots in the Hebrew Scripture. In this chapter we have already looked at the great Shema command given in Deuteronomy. In that great command the people are called to serve God wholeheartedly, and they are called to remember this command by writing it on their head and on their hand. The number 666 is likely connected to a description of the wealth of Solomon from the book of 1 Kings. When the queen of Sheba comes to see for herself the great wealth and power of Solomon, the book of 1 Kings says, "The weight of gold that came to Solomon in one year was six hundred sixty-six talents of gold, besides that which came from the traders and from the business of the merchants, and from all the kings of Arabia and the governors of the land" (1 Kings 10:14). Here, the acquisitiveness of Solomon is being described in such elaborate ways that the text causes Israel to remember Solomon as the king who replicated the political policies of empire belonging to Pharaoh.[6] It is also likely that in the number 666, each digit is intentionally one digit short of the number 777. The number seven is almost always used in the Bible to symbolize completion (for example, there are seven days in a week and seven years in the Sabbath cycle). In a sense, 666 is the ultimate number of incompletion. The gold Solomon was amassing is the symbolic number representing the end result of Israel's royal history. In particular, this number represents the attempts by Solomon and the other kings to find significance in the same ways other kingdoms find their significance and to achieve their power through the same oppressive means that other kingdoms use.

Put together, it is not difficult to understand the mark of the beast as a powerful apocalyptic symbol for the way those who are being conformed by the dominant culture reflect and are marked by its image. Put another way, one of the questions raised by the Revelator—and in the letter to the church in Pergamum in particular—is, do we as believers, being renewed into the image of God, wear the life of Shema or do our lives reflect the values and priorities of the empire?

The letter to the Pergamum church closes with a profound reference to hidden manna. "To everyone who conquers I will give some of the hidden manna" (Rev. 2:17). It is likely that this image is also used to present a sharp contrast between the life of dependence and trust the Israelites learned in the wilderness and the lure of King Nebuchadnezzar's table filled with fine food that was offered to the Hebrew children in the first chapter of Daniel. The Christians in Pergamum were being lured into the practices of the empire that at one level seemed somewhat harmless but were in reality beginning to form as well as conform them into the very image of the dominant culture. In the first Babylon, the Hebrew children had the discernment necessary to realize that sitting and dining at Nebuchadnezzar's table was about more than eating good food; it would make them the king's sons. What the church in Pergamum needed was a Spirit-empowered discernment that would help keep them from being conformed to the second Babylon and would enable them to live in the world without being of it.

Between Ephesus and Pergamum

The contemporary church is often plagued with the spirit of accommodation. I have intentionally not named examples of contemporary accommodation in this chapter. As a pastor I usually find myself caught between one group of people who believe me to be soft on sin because I do not name a laundry list of sins that the church often believes to be the most highly offensive to God and another group of people who think I over preach on several "isms," such as materialism, consumerism, nationalism, racism, sexism, and individualism. As a pastor I find myself caught between Ephesus and Pergamum. On the one hand, there are some subjects that I feel we tend to preach to the converted, and in so doing we, like Ephesus, become boundary keepers who put a big invisible sign on the front lawn of the church that says, "If you have committed the following sins or struggle with the following things, don't bother attending." But on the other hand, I am fearful of the many ways we compromise with the dominant practices of the culture and, like Pergamum, forsake the image of God for the image of the beast.

The book of Revelation essentially ends with the fall of Babylon in chapters 18 and 19. Chapter 18 describes how the kings, merchants, seafarers, and all those who found their identity in the empire weep and mourn and wail when Babylon is no more. They cry aloud because all that they identified their life with and found value in is no more. All the forces that had formed and conformed their character now lay in ashes. On the other side, chapter 19 describes the praise that goes up from the saints of heaven because their identity is not found in the empire but in the eternal kingdom of the Lamb. Although they had lived and worked in Babylon, it had never truly become their home. Those who rejoice in eternity are those who have found the discernment to live in the world but not be of the world, those whose lives reflect the light and love of the Lamb. Their values, identity, and convictions have formed in them not the image of the empire but the image of God. It is a difficult task, and we are enabled only by the power of the Spirit, but as believers we are called to dwell in a neighborhood somewhere between Ephesus and Pergamum.

Questions for Group Discussion

1. In what ways is the contemporary church tempted to accommodate to the culture?
2. When does the church "look like the Lamb but speak like the dragon"?
3. How can leaders in the church model what it means to live between Ephesus and Pergamum?

4

Thyatira

The Spirit of Privatized Faith

"And to the angel of the church in Thyatira write: . . . I
have this against you: you tolerate that woman Jezebel,
who calls herself a prophet and is teaching and beguil-
ing my servants to practice fornication and to eat food
sacrificed to idols."

The lead headline of the *Los Angeles Times* sports page read "Eli's
Not Coming." Eli Herring, a six-foot eight-inch, three-hundred-
thirty-pound offensive tackle from Brigham Young University, had
the size, agility, and athleticism to attract attention from nearly every
NFL team but had no intention of playing professional football. Eli
was passing up his opportunity to continue playing a game he loved,
and certainly the chance to set up his family with financial security,
in order to become a math teacher. Why? Because Eli Herring is a
devout Mormon who simply won't play football on Sunday. "If they
ever change to Saturdays, I'd be very interested," he said.[1]

Eli's story made the front page of the *Los Angeles Times* because the Raiders, while respecting Herring's beliefs, selected him in the sixth round of the 1995 NFL draft and tried to persuade him to join the team. It was believed that if Herring had not made teams aware of his decision in advance, he would have been chosen as early as the second round, because he was rated by most football prognosticators as one of the top five offensive linemen graduating from college that year. The Raiders offered him a three-year contract worth $1.5 million, not counting a healthy signing bonus and several performance incentives. He chose instead to honor the Sabbath and make twenty-two thousand dollars a year as a teacher.

The Raiders sent several coaches and former players, including two or three who were Mormon, to try to persuade Eli to play, but he politely declined. "Sunday is a day to go to church, instead of a working day," he said. "It's a day to spend with family. It's a day to remember the Lord. It's a day to get away from worldly things and refocus. That's what's important to me. I think people need role models. Playing in the NFL is a good way to be a role model. But more important is the strict observance of the Sabbath. This was a big opportunity for me to provide for my family, but it was not big enough for me to do something I felt was wrong in terms of the Lord."[2]

When Eli first made his decision not to play professional football, he kept it secret because he was afraid that people, including some in his own family, would think that he had gone crazy. Many, including his college coach and his own father, were not sure he was making the right decision. But Eli did not back down. When the author of the article checked in with Eli a few months after the draft, he was living in a small apartment in Utah, driving a thirteen-year-old Nissan with 199,000 miles on it, preparing to have a baby with his wife, teaching math, and working as an assistant coach for the high-school football team.

Like most who read the article, I was shocked that someone would intentionally choose *not* to play a professional sport. I'm unaware of another example of someone making the front page of a major newspaper's sports section for willfully deciding not to play. But I was more deeply troubled by my own reaction to the article. The first time I read Eli's story I was a seminary student who had made some fairly significant financial sacrifices myself to be obedient to what I believed to be God's will for my life. Yet I still found myself thinking as I read the article, "Come on, Eli. I mean, really. Your faith is one thing, but this is a chance to play professional football in the NFL." As I have reflected honestly over the years about my gut reaction to Eli's story, I have realized that my shock at his decision is not due simply to obvious theological differences regarding faith or even what Sabbath observance looks like. Rather, when I explore my deepest levels of conviction, I fear that although I give lip service to my Christian faith as primary, there are other values that are deeper priorities. I find too often that I seek first the kingdom of God and its righteousness as long as it doesn't cost me something "really important." I certainly don't think I'm alone in that struggle.

If you have ever watched gangster movies, at some point in the film one of the mob members (usually the godfather) will be forced to order the killing of someone who had previously been a close associate and perhaps even a family member. Before condemning the person to "sleep with the fishes," the mob boss will say this line: "It's not personal, it's business." In other words, the person who is about to take the life of another is saying, "If we lived in a world where only interpersonal relationships mattered, I would never do this; but we do not live in that kind of world, we live in a world primarily determined by business." I think part of the reason for the success of mob-based movies and television programs is due to the fact that we are deeply fascinated by the obvious dichotomy created for those who live in a mobster's world: radical social commitments and intimate cultural ties that must operate within a self-centered criminal value system shaped by an insensitivity to graphic violence. We are both shocked and fascinated by people who are able to divide their commitments in such a profound way that they can say with all seriousness, "It's not personal, it's business."

The church in Thyatira also found itself divided between its spiritual convictions and the economic pressures of the surrounding culture. Perhaps we can summarize the problem for the church in Thyatira with a play on the godfather's phrase. The spirit of the church in Thyatira was one that tended to say, "It's not *spiritual*, it's *business*."

Thyatira: A City of Guilds

The letter to the church in Thyatira is the longest and in some ways most difficult of the seven letters. It is interesting that this is the longest letter, given the fact that of the seven cities addressed in the letters of Revelation Thyatira was the least impressive politically and economically. Located at a significant crossroads, the city began as a military outpost. Conspicuous for having access to the natural materials necessary for manufacturing bronze, the artisans of the city became well known for making impressive weapons. The reputation of this resilient and brilliant bronze may be part of the reason why this letter is voiced by the one "whose feet are like burnished bronze" (Rev. 2:18). When Rome rose to power, the city was no longer needed as a military stronghold, so it turned its attention to business. Although Thyatira did not reach its peak of prosperity until the second and third centuries CE, at the time of John's writing the city would have been growing rapidly, as were the challenges faced by the church.

As Thyatira became a center for business, it also became the center for a number of trade guilds. Historians and archaeologists are aware of guilds existing in Thyatira for wool workers, linen workers, garment manufacturers, dyers, tanners, potters, bakers, slave dealers, and bronze smiths.[3] Like a modern-day chamber of commerce or trade union, these various guilds represented all the different industries of the day. One had to belong to one of these guilds to participate fully in the economic life around Thyatira.

The guilds became places that were both secular and religious in nature. On a business level, artisans and laborers would gather together as a guild to share stories, compare sales figures, exchange trade secrets, and the such. These trade guilds, however, were also dedicated to particular pagan deities. It is possible that one of the primary deities honored by the guilds in Thyatira was Apollo. Apollo was believed to be the divine guardian of the city and the patron god of many of the city's trade guilds. "We know that the people of Thyatira believed that the Roman emperor was the incarnation of Apollo. In that city both Apollo and Caesar were acclaimed 'son of Zeus'—'son of the high god.'"[4]

It would be almost impossible for citizens of Thyatira to participate in the economy of the city without also participating in the guild meetings. Thus it appears that this letter centers on the very important question of whether the Christians of Thyatira could participate in these meetings. Complicating the question of guild participation was the fact that the guild meals would often turn into raucous quasi-worship celebrations. The guild feast would usually begin with a cup of wine poured out as a libation and an offering to the gods. Highly influenced by the moral and sexual laxity of Roman culture, these events were almost always filled with drunken partying, in the spirit of "what happens at the guild stays at the guild."

The difficult decision for Christians in a city like Thyatira was how much of pagan society to accept and how much to condemn. These everyday, pragmatic questions were difficult, urgent, and significant. Not surprisingly, almost every New Testament epistle addresses some of these everyday questions: What should believers wear? What may they eat? How should they eat? Who can they talk to? Who should they marry? What should they do with their property? What relationship should they have with slaves and the institution of slavery? How do believers live in the secularized economic world of Thyatira but not be of it? It appears that the general tendency of the early believers was to follow most social customs except in cases where idolatrous and immoral behaviors were obvious, and in those situations the tendency was to avoid attendance or participation. As Ramsay states:

> So far as we can gather, the rule laid down by St. Paul, and the practice of the Church, was that only in quite exceptional, rare cases should open disapproval of the customs of society be expressed; in many cases, where the idolatrous connection was not obvious, but only veiled or remote, the Christian might (and perhaps even ought to) comply with the usual forms, unless his attention was expressly called by any one of the guests to the idolatrous connection. . . . Hence there was a general tendency among the Christians to avoid situations, offices, and paths of life in which the performance of idolatrous ceremonial was necessary; and on this account they were generally stigmatized as morose, hostile to existing society, and deficient in active patriotism, if not actually disloyal.[5]

The Christians of Thyatira faced a very real problem regarding the guilds. If Christian merchants were members of a guild and participated fully in guild life, their material and financial interests were secure; but if they refused to participate in the guild's ceremonies, they were potentially committing economic suicide and would very soon be faced with exclusion from trade, poverty, and even bankruptcy. As William Barclay states, "The problem which faced every Christian in Thyatira was whether they were to make money or to be Christians."[6]

The letter to the church in Thyatira is, ironically, both comforting and disturbingly modern. It is comforting to know that finding the answers to everyday questions that seem to divide the sacred and the secular is not a new challenge. But like the church in Thyatira, I fear that we might find the Revelator's answers to our everyday questions far more challenging than we would like. Not long ago a Christian friend called me to ask my pastoral opinion regarding his difficult work situation. This person was a very gifted salesperson for a highly profitable company. When high-profile clients would come to town, it was my friend's responsibility to make sure they had a good time so that they would buy a lot of his company's products. The usual routine when clients came to town was for my friend to pick them up at the airport, check them into a nice hotel, take them to whichever sporting event the company had tickets for that evening, and then take them to the bar or strip club of their choice. All of this wining and dining is a fairly standard business practice used to set up the big sale at the meeting the following morning. My friend, who is very committed to living the holy life God desires, was torn apart with guilt and with questions regarding how to succeed in today's business culture without becoming part of "the world." How can he witness to a different kind of life while supporting the often exploitative and shadowy practices of business?

My friend's Thyatiran dilemma is not an isolated example. Over the years in ministry I have prayed with Christian restaurant owners struggling with the fact that they not only need to permit but also need to push liquor sales because it is their primary area of profit, with employees conflicted about the ethics of their companies, with women and men dealing with sexism and a high level of inappropriate sensuality in the workplace, and the like. The church I currently pastor is adjacent to the Hollywood industry. Thus many believers in my congregation are actors who wrestle daily with acting roles they aren't sure they should take, musicians who wonder whether they should sing a certain type of music or play in a certain kind of club, composers who aren't sure what to do when they are invited to create music for morally questionable film projects, and the list goes on and on. Christian young people deal with questions of clothing styles, parties to attend, and entertainments to participate in or to avoid. These are Thyatira questions. Is life spiritual, or is it business? Is it possible for us to divide life in such a way that the sacred and secular can be separated from each other so that faith can be a private matter and business a public one?

Jezebel: Dividing Body and Soul

Apparently in Thyatira there was a woman the Revelator names as "Jezebel" who had acquired influence in the congregation as a kind of prophetess. In the Old Testament, Jezebel was Ahab's queen who supported idolatry (1 Kings 16:31), thus leading the people of God astray. John seems to believe that the Jezebel of Thyatira was doing the same thing as the Old Testament queen because she was teaching her followers to "eat food sacrificed to idols" (Rev. 2:20). The Revelator condemned the church in Thyatira because it had allowed an unhealthy tolerance of her evil teaching and had refused to deal with her. We can presume that this Jezebel, like the Nicolaitans of Ephesus before her, was arguing that Christians could join a guild and participate in its feasts without compromising the faith. It is important to note that apparently her presence and her arguments were not obviously out-of-bounds for the believers. In fact, her statements were likely drawn from the dominant worldview of the day and were based on a Greek understanding of the relationship of the body and soul.

Greek philosophers, such as Plato and Socrates, considered the body and the soul to be separate entities. Plato, for example, believed that the physical and spiritual sides of the self are in a bad marriage that poorly combines within the human person the temporal and the eternal. The body, for the Greeks, is changing, decaying, and temporary, while the soul is eternal, unchanging, and immortal. Socrates believed that it is our soul that longs for the higher and eternal things, but it is weighed down by the imperfections and material longings of the body. For most of the ancient Greek philosophers, the soul preexisted the body and at death is finally freed to either migrate to another body for further purification or be eternally and gratefully freed from the bondage of mortality.

As the gospel increasingly reached into gentile Roman cultures influenced by this Hellenistic view of the body and soul, this dualistic worldview began to have an impact on the way the message of salvation was heard. While present-day study of the New Testament church tends to focus on the parts of the Jewish law that were left behind as the gospel spread to the gentiles, there were significant new influences on the gospel as well. Expectations for eternal life, for example, became increasingly understood and imagined in Greek rather than in Hebrew philosophical terms. Most importantly for the letter to the church in Thyatira, ideas of spiritual formation or discipleship were sometimes interpreted through the lens of physical and spiritual dualism, thus opening up new questions for the faith.

If we assume the influence of some form of Greek dualism, the likely argument of Thyatira's Jezebel was along the following lines: The rituals of the guilds aren't really meaningful even to the pagans; they are simply empty rituals. Although the pagan guild members may believe that the gods exist, Christians know that the gods are nothing, thus when believers participate in these cultic practices they are really worshiping nothing. Participation in the guild meetings gives Christians the opportunity to be witnesses to, or positive influences on, others. If believers do not participate in the guild events they will not only be persecuted and excluded, they will lose all relevance in the city and the economy. But most importantly, what God primarily cares about is the spirit or soul of the believer. If the soul of the believer is okay with the Lord, then one can choose to do whatever one likes with the temporal body.

Although the philosophical aspect of this argument may seem distant to us today, the dualistic split between the spiritual and secular is not. The spirit of privatized faith is prevalent in the church. I heard a political candidate say recently, "I am a person of deep faith, but I don't allow those faith convictions to influence my political agenda." That is a statement that clearly illustrates the demarcation between secular and sacred that runs through the heart of many believers and many churches. In North America, faith is seen as a very important private commitment, but at the same time, it is a commitment that seems to have less and less influence on the economic, political, and public decisions we face.

The Revelator has several responses to this kind of dualism. "I gave her time to repent, but she refuses to repent of her fornication" (2:21). The one who "has eyes like a flame of fire" (2:18) is merciful even to Jezebel and has given her time to repent; yet she remains unfaithful. It is possible, given the sexual nature of the guild festivities, to take the inference to fornication literally. It is far more likely, however, that John is joining the Old Testament prophets, who compared the people of God to an unfaithful spouse. Those who practiced idolatry in the Old Testament, such as Hosea's wife, Gomer, were viewed as "whoring themselves" to other gods. "When Israel was unfaithful and untrue to God, it was as if she broke the marriage vow which existed between herself and God."[7] Thyatira's Jezebel was leading the people into covenantal infidelity to God.

It is interesting that the threat to the church's faithfulness came from within rather than from outside the church. As Barclay states, "It was not the threat of persecution; it did not come from the panoply of heathen worship; it did not come from the state insistence on caesar worship. It came from inside the Church; it came from those within the Church who proposed to face the world with the most dangerous of all doctrines, a doctrine of compromise."[8]

Through John the Revelator, Christ speaks words of judgment concerning this Jezebel: "Beware, I am throwing her on a bed, and those who commit adultery with her I am throwing into great distress, unless they repent of her doings; and I will strike her children dead" (2:22–23). It is most likely that the bed on which Jezebel will be thrown is a reference to the banquet couches on which those who attended the guild feasts would have reclined. The image here is quite stark. The couches or beds that are currently associated with partying and wild living will instead become associated with the distress and brokenness for Jezebel and her children—those who are following her teaching.

It is also possible to read the judgment on Thyatira's idolatry literally. Like Ananias and Sapphira in Acts 5, the divine judgment might take away the life of the disobedient, but it is more likely that the seeds of destruction are woven into the very acts of disobedience themselves. One does not need to look very far to discover how trying to serve two gods adversely affects family dynamics, political systems, individual psyches, and even the natural world. When Jezebel and her children do not repent, some form of brokenness, dysfunction, and death is always the consequence.

The Revelator praises some in the church of Thyatira for holding fast and not giving in to the lure of Jezebel. "To the rest of you in Thyatira, who do not hold this teaching, who have not learned what some call 'the deep things of Satan,' to you I say, I do not lay on you any other burden. . . . [Instead] I will give authority over the nations; to rule them with an iron rod, as when clay pots are shattered" (Rev. 2:24, 26–27). It is possible that "the deep things of Satan" refers to the heresy of Gnosticism that posed an immense challenge to the faith of the early church. Not only were the Gnostics radical dualists who elevated the eternal soul and lowered the temporal body, but they also declared that a secret knowledge (*gnosis* in the Greek) was needed to free the soul from the body and allow it to enter into the realm of the eternal. It very well could be that Jezebel was offering a form of Gnosticism that not only freed people to do whatever they wished with their bodies but also promised a special knowledge or depth of insight not available to all.

This kind of teaching was treacherously persuasive for the early church, but Christ promises, "To the one who conquers I will also give the morning star" (2:28). William Barclay points out that this mention of the morning star may be a reference to the hope of the resurrection that every believer shares, or it may be the promise of Christ himself. In Revelation 22:16 the risen Christ declares, "I am . . . the bright morning star." Therefore, "The man who is faithful unto death will receive the greatest prize of all—he will receive no other and no less than Jesus Christ Himself."[9]

Scripture and the Body

Scripture does not hold to the kind of distinction between soul and body or spiritual and sacred that the apparently Hellenized Jezebel was proclaiming.[10] The Old Testament begins with a creation hymn that in each of its seven stanzas affirms the goodness of creation. God pronounced as "good" every physical thing that he created. Unlike dualistic worldviews, such as those of the Gnostics and Hellenists, the Old Testament does not view material reality in negative terms. Physical, material reality is the good creation of a loving Father.

We also discover in the creation story that the Hebrews viewed the person as being deeply connected to the stuff of earth. Adam is literally created from the dust of the ground. So, although as I argued in the introduction that every human being is more than the sum of his or her material parts, the human person—as a person—is inextricably linked to their physical body. There is an essence, spirit, or soul that emerges within people that makes them uniquely in creation the image of God, but this spiritual or soul-ish aspect of the human person is intimately interwoven with and related to our physical being.

Because the Hebrew worldview is not dualistic, death is neither a relief nor a blessing as it was for Plato or Socrates; it is instead an enemy to the way God wants things to be. Although creatures die, the uniqueness of humankind is such that death is not necessarily the end of their story. Usually, in the Old Testament narratives, the dead go to a place of rest—Sheol—where they await the redemption of all things that God will enact through his people, and most importantly through his Messiah. When God redeems and restores all things, that redemption will include the resurrection of the dead, at which time the spiritual essence of a person will be united (in some sense reunited) with a resurrected and now incorruptible body. When redemption takes place, "the earth will be full of the knowledge of the LORD as the waters cover the sea" (Isa. 11:9; cf. Hab. 2:14). It is important to note in these Hebrew expectations that although they believed that people maintain a kind of spiritual existence after death, this spiritual existence is only temporary as they wait to be re-embodied. The hopes of the Hebrew people were always for eternal postresurrection embodied living.

Jesus also came in the fleshly form of humanity and shockingly did not proclaim the coming of the kingdom of God (or kingdom of heaven) as solely a future event. Instead he proclaimed that the kingdom had indeed arrived, through him. It is unlikely that the believers in the early church thought of heaven as "in the sky." They viewed heaven as being invisibly present or even adjacent to the material and visible world. For example, in Revelation 4, when John gets a glimpse into the throne room of heaven, although he steps *up* into God's presence he probably does not envision God reigning from somewhere high above in the heavens but more like the way C. S. Lewis's mythical kingdom of Narnia is accessible through the wardrobe. The kingdom of God exists all around us and is revealed as present and visible in the signs and ministry of Jesus.

Jesus's death was a great shock to the disciples. The disciples had readily accepted the idea that Jesus was Messiah, but what was highly problematic for them was that the Messiah died. Without question their expectation was that the Messiah would build the kingdom and establish it by conquering all of the kingdom's enemies. Instead he was crucified. Undoubtedly the definitive moment for the disciples was the resurrection of Jesus. Their Jewish hopes had been fulfilled but in a way that was very different from what they had imagined. Jesus rose again from the dead as the "first fruits" of the present and coming eternal kingdom of God.

All of this is important because it puts in context what the early church really believed about the relationship of the body to the human spirit or soul. The early church was caught between a materialistic view of the body (a view that espouses that we eat, drink, and be merry because tomorrow we are dead) and the Greek and Gnostic view of the body, which carried with it the idea of the immortality of the soul and the denigration of the temporal body. This is the philosophical idea that leads to Jezebel's teaching: our eternal and immortal souls are at peace with God so we can now do whatever we want to or need to with our temporal and decaying bodies.

Paul and the early church leaders, like their Hebrew forebears in the faith, believed in the goodness of the body, but they did not see the body as an end in itself. Although they believed that a person is not just a material being, they believed that our assurance (and our model) of eternal life was revealed and guaranteed in the bodily resurrection of Jesus from the dead.

Certainly the resurrection of Jesus freed the early church from the fear of death. Death had forever lost its "sting." This had several consequences. First, the principalities and powers no longer had authority over the early Christians. The threat caesar carried in his hand was the threat of death, but because the early believers no longer feared death they could become martyrs—witnesses—to and for the kingdom of God. Secondly, they also became well known for their care of the sick. In ancient cultures the sick—especially those with deadly and communicable diseases—were removed from society. The church, however, is commanded to gather around and lay hands on the sick. Their lack of fear regarding death gave them the ability to embrace and care for the sick in ways that also witnessed to God's kingdom.

Of particular importance for our understanding of this letter is that the resurrection gave the early church a hope in what we might call the life *after* life *after* death. Although the church believed deeply in immediate life after death in the presence of the Lord, this was not thought to be the final destiny for which the Christian is bound. This state of immediate life after death is one in which the dead are held firmly within the conscious love of God and the conscious presence of Jesus while they await the day of redemption (Rev. 6:9–11). The ultimate hope is that there will be a new (or renewed) creation and that the dead will be raised in ways that are congruent with but at the same time completely different from our current embodied life. In the judgment, all that does not belong to the kingdom will be destroyed, but all that was established in and for the kingdom will be eternal. Thus the work that is done in the body for the kingdom of God establishes that which is eternal. Although the final hope is for an incorruptible body (1 Cor. 15), it is still a body nonetheless. One can't separate the soul from the body in the way Thyatira's Jezebel would like because humankind is so uniquely linked to embodiment that our lives will always have some form of corporeal existence.

Thus Paul in particular implores believers to "glorify God in your body" (1 Cor. 6:20) and prays that our "spirit and soul and body be kept sound and blameless at the coming of our Lord Jesus Christ" (1 Thess. 5:23). Biblical hope never completely separates the soul from the body, and so there can be no dichotomy between the sacred and the secular for the believer.

The problem for Jezebel and the Christians of Thyatira, then, is that God doesn't divide our lives into the physical and the spiritual or the sacred and the secular. God doesn't allow us to segment our lives in that way. We don't get to say, this is the business part of my life, this is my family part, this is my spiritual part, and so on. Although we at times may assume different roles or responsibilities, God sees our lives as a unified whole. Thus one can't say to God, "It's not spiritual, it's business," because it all belongs to him.

Lot and Zacchaeus

The life that is in the world and not of it is certainly not easy. There is a unique power of the Spirit necessary to practice the discernment required by Scripture. On the one side the church must guard against the instinct to sectarianism that desires to be separated from all that is in the world. There are many examples throughout history of people who formed isolated communities of "the faithful" and cut themselves off from the rest of the world. The Thyatiran Christians are not called to be isolated from the day-to-day economy of life in the world. Yet they are strongly rebuked by the Spirit for the ways they have been participating in and also the ways in which—through Jezebel—they have been shaped by the world. How does one learn to live in the world but not be of it?

I wish Scripture gave us three or four principles clearly laid out for how to discern the world, but instead it usually gives us narratives or stories to contemplate. Let me use two contrasting stories as models for thinking about living with and without a privatized faith.

The first story is from one who did not discern the world. In Genesis 13 Abraham and his nephew Lot divide their clans. Scripture tells us that Abraham and Lot's families were getting too large to coexist in one place, and so Abraham willingly divided the land. He took Lot and showed him both sides of the land. "Lot looked about him, and saw that the plain of the Jordan was well watered everywhere like the garden of the LORD, like the land of Egypt, in the direction of Zoar" (Gen. 13:10). We are then told that Abraham settled in the land of Canaan, while Lot settled among the cities on the plain and moved his tent as far as the wicked city of Sodom.

The life of Lot and his family is picked up again in chapter 19. Now Lot is not just living near the city, he is "sitting in the gateway of Sodom" (19:1). There are two possible reasons for Lot's presence in the gateway. Lot has either become an official in the city of Sodom and so sits at the gate dispensing judgment for those who come to the gate with disputes, or he is at the entrance of the city doing business at the place where the market was most likely located. Either way, it is clear that in six short chapters Lot and his family have become tied to the city and its values.

The story of the destruction of the city of Sodom and its profound effect on Lot's life is well known, but there are two or three tragic aspects to consider. Certainly the most famous loss for Lot is the transformation of his wife into a pillar of salt. Although the messengers of the Lord tell Lot and his family not to turn around, Lot's wife does turn around to behold the destruction of the city and turns into a pillar of salt. We are not explicitly told her motivation for turning, although it is generally inferred that she turns because a part of her is now tied to and drawn to the city of Sodom. She is destroyed along with the city because there is now more of her identity informed by being of the world than being simply in it. Another troubling part of this story is when Lot tells the men pledged to be married to his daughters that they should leave the city because God is going to destroy it and they do not believe him because "he seemed to his sons-in-law to be jesting" (19:14). And certainly most horrific of all is when his daughters "who have not known a man" (19:8) demonstrate that they too have learned much from the city by getting their father intoxicated and lying with him so that they might have offspring (19:30–38).

The horrific story of Lot's demise was kept by the people of Israel because they wanted their children to remember the danger of establishing one's life too close to the value systems of empire. For centuries the story of Lot has been relived again and again in the church of privatized faith. Like Lot, the church too often stands at the top of the hill and chooses the luxurious life of the empire because, "It's not spiritual, it's business."

Yet, something in us realizes that all of life is spiritual. Zacchaeus serves as a kind of anti-Lot in Scripture. Whereas Lot represents the righteous person who gets caught up in the secular, Zacchaeus represents the worldly person who is captured by the sacred. When in Luke 19 Zacchaeus encounters Jesus over dinner, there is no record of

Jesus doing anything more than eating dinner at Zacchaeus's house. And yet when faced with the convicting presence of Christ, Zacchaeus vows to give back half of his possessions, to assist the poor, and to compensate fully those whom he has defrauded. The call of Christ is a call that captures all of Zacchaeus's life.

William Herzog provides a very interesting interpretation of the parable that immediately follows the story of Zacchaeus. The parable of the pounds is usually interpreted to mean that we are all given certain talents and abilities from God and that we will each be held accountable for how we use those abilities to further the power and purposes of God's kingdom. Herzog, however, interprets the parable as a way of describing what happened to Zacchaeus when he returned to work the day after meeting with Jesus to let his employers know that he was no longer going to participate in their systems of exploitation. In the parable, argues Herzog, the third servant who buries his pound and then gives it back to the power-grabbing master serves as a kind of "whistle-blower" against the systems of usury that not only typified the economy of the first century but also would have been very similar to the methods of taxation that Zacchaeus would have been using prior to his encounter with Jesus.[11] For Herzog, the parable serves as a reminder of the kind of holistic commitment Zacchaeus was making to Christ, and it also serves as a reminder of the potential costs that commitment would likely entail.

The problem with the spirit of privatized faith is that it robs the church of its ability to become a contrast model to the world in every area of life. The church is called to be a unique people—resident aliens—in a world shaped by different values and convictions. Privatized faith gives cognitive assent to a different kingdom but fails to witness to that kingdom's presence.

Often when I am preaching I get the sense that people in the congregation are saying "amen" as I declare the values of God's kingdom, but possessed as we so often are in North America by a spirit of privatized faith, we often walk out the doors of the sanctuary and say, "The Word of the Lord was quite stirring today, but now as we go back into the 'real world' we will have to return to the way things truly are." The fateful destruction for Lot occurred when Sodom became the "real world" and God's covenantal life became an idealistic concept. Salvation came to Zacchaeus when the kingdom of Christ became the "real world" for him.

The church that is doing battle with the spirit of privatized faith is learning to pray, "Thy kingdom come and Thy will be done, on earth as it is in heaven," as it is also learning to embody together the reality that "the kingdom of this world has become the kingdom of our Lord, and of His Messiah" (Rev. 11:15).

Questions for Group Discussion

1. What does the temptation of Jezebel sound like in the world today?
2. In what ways does the contemporary culture (and the contemporary church) treat faith as private?
3. What are some of the major ways that Christians struggle to live out a faith that encompasses all of life?

5

Sardis

The Spirit of Apathetic Faith

"And to the angel of the church in Sardis write: . . . I know your works; you have a name of being alive, but you are dead. Wake up, and strengthen what remains."

It had taken us five years of marriage, but Debbie and I had saved enough to buy about 1300 square feet of Southern California property. We were not only happy first-time homeowners, but we also believed that we had been very cautious ones. Having been thoroughly terrified by the Tom Hanks movie *The Money Pit* (I still laugh until I cry every time I see the scene when the bathtub falls through the floor and Tom can't stop his crazy-person laugh), we made sure that legions of inspectors examined the house before we signed on the dotted line. We had termite inspectors, earthquake engineers, structural specialists, and electricians all give us the thumbs-up on the quality and safety of the house, and most importantly our investment. We were thrilled to be homeowners.

Everything was fine for about two weeks. I was up late one night when I heard what sounded like all kinds of scratching going on above my head. It then sounded like someone had installed a tiny bowling alley above the ceiling as round objects kept rolling back and forth. I assumed that perhaps a squirrel had accidentally gotten stuck in the attic and was scurrying around with its stockpile of nuts trying to find a way out. When the sounds were gone in the morning I hoped that it had found an escape. But the next night the sounds returned, only now I noticed they were going on in more than one room. They returned the next night, and the next, and the next.

We called a rodent expert (one of the few experts not to have examined the house ahead of time), who proceeded to inform us that we had a tree rat problem. Prior to his inspection I was unaware of the existence of tree rats, but he informed us that Southern California is full of them. With a tug on his low-riding waist band, he pointed to the many palm trees in our neighborhood where apparently many generations of tree rats dwell, only to come out at night in search of food and entertainment. He pointed out how the two-inch gaps in the eaves on our house were typical of homes built in the 1920s and were put there to allow ventilation in the attic. Unfortunately they also served as perfect entry points for tree rats to have free reign of the attic. He suggested several areas in the eaves where we could put mesh to try to keep out our nightly visitors.

That night Debbie and I lay in bed with the curtains open and looked toward the trees. Our bedroom was in the back of the house, giving us unimpeded visual confirmation of the invasion about to take place. Sure enough, about 10:30 pm or so the trees started swinging. With a high-powered flashlight in hand I spotlit rodent after rodent running across the power wires and the branches of the trees in the backyard, jumping down onto the roof, and then disappearing through various holes in the eaves. Debbie and I were both quite disturbed by our uninvited night guests.

Debbie put me to work the next day installing mesh over the vents near the roof line where the rats were finding easy access. Although I tried various sizes of mesh material, the tree rats seemed to find ways of creating a hole, pulling back a corner, or finding an access point I hadn't discovered. Having been warned against poisoning them—the only thing worse than a live rat in your attic is a dead one—I tried trapping them. I was successful a couple of times, but I soon discovered that even though I bought the largest traps available, many of the rats were so big that they would either carry off the traps or get stuck just enough that I would then be responsible for doing things a city boy like myself was not prepared to do.

It took several failed attempts to get rid of our problem before we finally found the solution. We moved to Oklahoma.

Sardis: The Fortified City

Sardis was a prosperous city that by the end of the first century had seen better days. Of the seven cities mentioned, Sardis was the most protected. The cliff on which the city was built gave it only one major access route and thus made the gates of the city easy to protect. When armies tried to attack the city they were always pushed away.

The city of Sardis had never been taken captive by direct assault. But twice in its history, once in 549 BCE and again in 195 BCE, it had been conquered and its leader deposed by enemies who found a "chink in the armor." The cliffs were scaled and a way into the city was found through a small access hole in the wall. In both cases, while the city slept in the knowledge that its gates were secure, the citizens of Sardis awoke to find that they were under surprise attack. In 549, Cyrus captured Sardis by sending a climber up a crevice on one of the nearly perpendicular cliffs on one side of the city. In 195, Lagoras of Crete led fifteen men through the same entry point, opened the gates of the city from within, and allowed the armies of Antiochus the Great to capture the sleeping city.[1] In the poetry and wisdom literature of the day, Sardis became synonymous with the dangers of overconfidence, pride, and arrogance. The history of Sardis demonstrated the need to be aware of enemies who come "like a thief in the night" (Rev. 3:3).

By the first century the glory days of Sardis were in the past. In the sixth century BCE it was the capital city of the kingdom of Lydia and later a center of Persian government. Although Sardis was no longer a major power center, it was still the meeting place of several trade routes, and it prospered from the fertile valley that lay below it. Ramsay describes it as, "A city of the past, a relic of the period of barbaric warfare, which lived rather on its ancient prestige than on its suitability to present conditions."[2] The people of Sardis were well known in the time of the Revelator for their luxurious and loose way of life. It was a city of decadence. Of it Gonzalez writes, "All in all, it probably was a comfortable but unexciting place to live."[3]

The Revelator's letter to the church in Sardis is rather brief; however, when it is contrasted with the other letters, we find that we may learn as much from what is *not* included in this letter as we do from what is included. Unlike the letters to the other six churches, this letter contains no mention of persecution, no reference to the danger of heresy, and no allusion to Jewish opposition to the church. It would appear that the church in Sardis is unique among the seven churches in that it is not faced with any of the trials of its sister congregations. The words of the Revelator, "I know your works; you have a name of being alive, but you are dead" (3:1), paint a "picture of nominal Christianity, outwardly prosperous, busy with the externals of religious activity, but devoid of spiritual life and power."[4] Like many churches, the church in Sardis had apparently learned to coast on its past glories and achievements with the sort of assurance that the sentinels guarding the gate of Sardis must have felt before the city was taken by surprise.

This is a picture of a church that is proud, bored, and living off its memory, but it is not moving forward. So the spirit of Sardis seems to be a spirit of apathetic faith that allows the church to look alive while in reality it is dead. In the church at Sardis there is nothing wrong, and yet everything is wrong.

This letter reminds me of the words of the prophet Ezekiel regarding the root sin of Sodom. As we have already seen in the story of Lot, Sodom is best known for its grotesque sexuality and obvious violence, but in Ezekiel 16 Israel is warned that they are not only participating in the sin of Sodom but also risking the judgment of Sodom:

> You not only followed their ways, and acted according to their abominations; within a very little time you were more corrupt than they in

all your ways. As I live, says the LORD GOD, your sister Sodom and her daughters have not done as you and your daughters have done. This was the guilt of your sister Sodom: she and her daughters had pride, excess of food, and prosperous ease, but did not aid the poor and needy. They were haughty, and did abominable things before me; therefore I removed them when I saw it. (Ezek. 16:47–50)

Sardis had the reputation of spiritual life and vitality, but in the sight of God it was dead. As Ramsay suggests, "The Church here is addressed, apparently with the set purpose of suggesting that the fortunes of ancient Sardis had been its own fortunes, that it had endured those sieges, committed those faults of carelessness and blind confidence, and sunk into the same decay and death as the city."[5] The church of Sardis was not alive enough to have enemies or confront heresy. It had simply become the model of nonoffensive Christian faith.

The unfortunate fate of the church of Sardis was that life had been too easy for it. A lack of challenge, a lack of threat, and a lack of tension from inside or outside the church had left it at peace, but as William Barclay points out, "it was the peace of the dead."[6]

Whenever I think about the church at Sardis I think about a church where a friend from seminary had served as an intern. The church building is an amazing structure that is well known in the city for its beauty and exquisite architecture. The property is a prime location with high visibility, easy access, and hundreds—if not thousands—of people living within walking distance of the church. The church is well endowed and so has all the financial wherewithal it needs to maintain the facility, pay the pastoral staff very well, and fund ministries. But the church is essentially dead. Every day of the week people come to take a tour of the facility, but every Sunday only a handful of older saints come to sit in the pews for worship. A nonprofit organization uses part of the church facility to give aid to the poor of the city, but while many find food for the day, the church reaches few with the bread of life.

The church in North America is blessed with a history of religious liberty and economic prosperity, but like the church in Sardis, the North American church is often afflicted with the spirit of apathetic faith. The church often has a name for being alive, but it is dead.

Five Imperatives

All is not lost in Sardis. The message to the church contains five urgent commands from the Lord of the churches. These imperatives are a gift of grace. If death were the final word for the church captured by the spirit of apathetic faith, no commands would be necessary, but the power of God that resurrected Jesus from the dead also makes it possible for the dead church to live again.

The first command is for the church to "wake up" (Rev. 3:2). A more literal translation of this command would be "keep watching." Given the city's history of vulnerability to surprise attack, this command seems particularly relevant for the church in Sardis. The Christians in Sardis were participating in what Lutheran scholar Gerhard Krodel calls "ecclesiastical sleepwalking."[7] But there is still time to wake up. The letter warns Sardis that the intruder it must prepare for is the Lord himself. "I will come like a thief," says the Lord, "and you will not know what hour I will come to you" (3:3). "Christ comes to rob them of the complacency that they mistake for true security."[8]

I greatly miss in my life a woman named Glaphré Gilliland, who before going to be with the Lord taught seminars on prayer and was an important spiritual advisor to many. She was my mother's room-mate in college and her lifelong best friend. Although she was extremely ill for the last decades of her life and more often than not homebound, she counseled hundreds of people in their walk with the Lord through letters and phone calls. When Glaphré and I would talk on the phone, she had an amazing spiritual sensitivity to profoundly speak a word from the Lord into various troubled situations and to hear through lies. She would usually ask the question, "Scott, how are you and God doing?" And there was no possible way that I could do anything but tell the truth.

Once when she asked me that question I said to her, "Glaphré, I'm doing okay. I mean, I think God and I are just fine. I would say that we are just coasting along through life together." There was a significant pause on the line. I knew she could sense the tentativeness in my answer and feel the spiritual apathy that was dominating my life at the time. She simply replied, "I will really be praying for you Scott, because as I'm sure you are aware, there is only one direction

a person can coast." Nothing else needed to be said. Since then her
words have haunted me during my own times of spiritual apathy
and have constantly reminded me that it is the Lord's desire for us
to be vigilant and awake in our spiritual lives, always prepared for
him to come and move us forward and shake us from our proneness
to spiritual apathy.

The second command to the church in Sardis is to "strengthen
what remains" (3:2). If the church was near the point of death, what
remained? Most likely it was the external forms of the Christian
life—worship, rituals, disciplines, practices, fellowship—that were
left in Sardis. We are often critical of the forms or structures of the
church's life together, and there are certainly important moments in
the life of the church when we should analyze the effectiveness and
relevancy of our routines. But it would appear that the Revelator is
not critical of the forms that remained in Sardis as much as he is wary
of the spirit in which they were lived out. What Sardis needed was
not a new form but a renewed filling of God's Spirit.

The church is called to, "Remember then what you received and
heard" (3:3). The remembering that Sardis needed to do was a special
kind of remembering. The kind of memory it had been keeping was a
glorification of the past. Living solely in the past often causes the church
to become stagnant as it dwells on all that has gone on before. The kind
of remembering Sardis needed to do was the recalling of the presence
of God that enlivened and gave power in the challenges of the past so
that they could have faith to move forward into God's future.

I am reminded here of the great faith chapter of Hebrews 11. In that
chapter the stories of the heroes of faith—Abel, Enoch, Noah, Abraham, Moses, Gideon, Barak, Samson, Jephthah, David, Samuel, and
the prophets—are recounted as part of the great cloud of witnesses
to the life of faith. But these models of faith are not remembered so
that the early church could glory in its past but so that it too could
"run with perseverance the race that is set before us, looking to Jesus
the pioneer and perfecter of our faith" (Heb. 12:1–2).

It is very easy for communities of faith to fall into the wrong kind
of remembering. The wondrous work of God in the past can often
become a point of reference not for future faith but for stagnant
reminiscing. Sometimes when I hear churches rehearse the great days

of their past I'm reminded of the words to Bruce Springsteen's song
Glory Days:

> Now I think I'm going down to the well tonight
> And I'm going to drink till I get my fill.
> And I hope when I get old I don't sit around thinking
>   about it,
> But I probably will.
> Yeah, just sitting back trying to recapture a little of the
>   glory of,
> Well time slips away and leaves you with nothing mister
> But boring stories of—glory days.

The stories of the church's glory days may take place in hallways and
board meetings rather than at "the well," but nevertheless the church is
called to a unique form of memory that does not simply dwell on God's
past work but remembers his power in order to help the congregation
fulfill the fourth command given in the letter to the church—to "obey"
what it has heard. Again, like the believers to whom Hebrews is written,
the church in Sardis needs to remember the great moments of faith in
the past so that they can "lift your drooping hands and strengthen your
weak knees, and make straight paths for your feet, so that what is lame
may not be put out of joint, but rather healed" (Heb. 12:12–13).

The church is next called to "repent" (Rev. 3:3). The letter to Sardis
makes reference to some "who have not soiled their clothes" but instead
"will walk with [the Lord] dressed in white" (3:4). Those, however,
who hear the word of the Lord and conquer the spirit of spiritual
apathy "will be clothed like them in white robes" (3:5). These references to white, clean garments are almost certainly connected to the
early church's practice of dressing believers in white robes as they left
the waters of baptism, symbolizing the beginning of the new life that
they had received in Christ. It is not too late for the apathetic church.
The change that they need to make is not radical; they simply need
to remember what they already are—new creations in Christ Jesus.
Like the reformer Martin Luther, who would cry out when he was
tempted, "I am baptized!" the church in Sardis needs to remember
what God had already formed it to be and return to the life of newness to which God had called it.

Tough Questions

In his book *The Present Future*, church consultant Reggie McNeal raises six tough questions for the church. Although each of his questions is important and relevant, there are four that are particularly relevant for the church possessed by the deadly apathetic spirit of Sardis.

McNeal asks how we are to deconvert the community of faith from what he calls "Church-ianity" to Christianity. "The church was created to be the people of God to join him in his redemptive mission in the world. The church was never intended to exist for itself. It was and is the chosen instrument of God to expand his kingdom."[9] The North American church, like the church of Sardis, can quickly become a kind of social club rather than the living and vital body of Christ in the world. The church can easily see its task to be maintaining its structures rather than fulfilling its divine mission. The danger of placing structures above reaching people—what McNeal refers to as a "hardening of the categories"—is not limited to the church, for we see the tendency to maintain structures far beyond their usefulness all around us, in systems of government, education, and economics.

It is interesting that in the Old Testament a law was given to mandate a periodical renewal of the system. The law of Jubilee—given in Leviticus 25—was a complete renewal of the economic system to be enacted every fiftieth year. The economic codes of Israel included several laws for social welfare. The gleaning laws mandated that people not harvest the edges of their fields so that the people were always prepared to assist the wanderer and sojourner in the land by making the rows closest to the road available for the needs of the stranger. Tithing laws were instituted not just to care for the Levites and the temple but also to create a pool of resources to care for the widows, orphans, and other needy people within the community. Sabbath laws applied to more than just the week, for on the seventh year the land, the beasts of burden, and laborers received a year of renewal in which the entire community shared life together in shalom. But even with these unique laws of justice shaping the economic system, the law of Jubilee seems to understand that even just systems need a do-over from time to time. So in the Year of Jubilee, all land was returned to its original owners and all debts were cancelled. In other words, the entire economic structure was reset so that individuals and families caught in systems and cycles of debt and oppression could begin anew.

Although the other economic codes of Israel were followed religiously, the people never enacted the year of Jubilee. Why? Well, that is not a difficult question to answer. Jubilee was never enacted because people who have power and wealth within the system are rarely willing to give up their status and position.

What is true of the economic system is also true of our religious systems. Denominations continue with administrative structures that are outdated and admittedly not efficient to help the church achieve its mission because people who have achieved power within a certain system find it difficult to give up that power. Discipleship practices grow stagnant in a church because certain people have always had a particular class or small group and find it too hard to move beyond their comfortable relationships. Styles of worship fail to meet the needs of those outside the church, but they fit the vocal training of the person who has always been the soloist. The list could go on. Having been a pastor for several years and having grown up in a parsonage, I can think of so many times when the mission of the church was secondary to "the way we've always done it." This is not just a laity problem, it is also my problem as a church leader. It is easy for all of us to become members of what McNeal calles "Church-ianity" rather than Christianity.[10] The church of Sardis could use a Jubilee in which structures take a back seat to mission, but it takes the Spirit of God to awaken us from our self-centeredness and to give us a willingness to repent of our apathy.

McNeal also believes that the church has to begin asking how it can transform its community or how it can hit the streets with the gospel. The church of Sardis had a tendency to believe that if we simply "build it, they will come." We are often lulled into believing that the practices of the past worked for us and so they should continue to work for others regardless of their culture and background. McNeal writes:

> The Pharisees' evangelism strategy (and the strategy of most people who have grown up in the church) . . . was "Come and get it!" In ad-

dition they had contorted God's message to moralism: "You people 'out there' need to straighten up!" . . . Their message to people outside the (Pharisee) bubble was: "Become like us (translated: believe like us, dress like us, vote like us, act like us, like what we like, don't like what we don't like). If you become like us (jump through cultural hoops and adopt ours), we will consider you for club membership." . . . (Instead) we need to go where people are already hanging out and be prepared to have conversations with them about the great love of our lives. This will require our shifting our efforts from growing churches into transforming communities.[11]

There is an old saying around the church that goes, "If we don't evangelize, we cannibalize." It is easy to picture the Sardis church as one in which infighting and bickering about things that are trivial— the cannibalizing of the saints—had replaced the desire to share their great love for Christ with others.

The church dominated by the spirit of apathetic faith also needs to be a church that learns to exegete the culture. Frequently, churches that have the appearance of being alive but are really dead have stopped trying to make the gospel relevant to the needs of the surrounding culture. Reggie McNeal wonders how long it will be until the church learns how to turn members into missionaries. There have been several studies done on the state of the American church that are less than optimistic.[12] A statistic that I find particularly disturbing from youth specialist Dawson McAlister is that 90 percent of students active in high school youth groups stop attending church by the time they are sophomores in college. Of that 90 percent, one-third will never return.[13] Although there are many reasons why the church is having difficulty keeping its young people, certainly one of the reasons for this loss is the perception that the church no longer speaks relevantly to the issues of the day. McNeal again writes:

I am amazed at how many congregations will cheer denominationally produced videos of foreign mission efforts that include contextualized worship experiences (native dance, native instruments) but, when the lights come on, rant against the same strategy in their clubhouse. . . . Missiologists know that people must worship God in their own heart language. North American church club members are quite willing to deny this privilege even to our own church kids in order to preserve the club culture.[14]

One last question that McNeal raises, a question that is critical for the church of Sardis, is how do we develop followers of Jesus? The apathetic church is looking for members while the missional church is developing disciples. It is the primary task of the church to create an environment where people are renewed in the image of God. The spirit of apathetic faith is present whenever the institution of the church becomes an end in itself. The church of Sardis is not the Way, the Truth, and the Life, it is the means through which people come to discover the one who is the Way, the Truth, and the Life. The life of the church is renewed inasmuch as we point people to the giver of life.

The Book of Life

The renewal of the Sardis church will most likely include risk. The Revelator, speaking for Christ, states that if the church can overcome its spirit of apathy, "I will not blot your name out of the book of life; I will confess your name before my Father and before his angels" (Rev. 3:5). It is quite possible that the reference to the "book of life" is an allusion to the citizenship registries that were common in the Roman world. Some scholars have suggested that the church in Sardis had gained acceptance in the culture by attempting to fit into the system and by, at times, denying the name of Christ.[15] It may be that the faithful few of Sardis faced having their citizenship removed, but Christ assures them that they will not be removed from the Father's book of life. However, the Spirit is calling them to seek kingdom citizenship first and to find their lives recorded in God's ongoing history.

I am reminded of the words of Jesus in the Sermon on the Mount about the church being called to be the light of the world and the salt of the earth. "But if the salt has lost its taste, how can its saltiness be restored? It is no longer good for anything, but is thrown out and trampled under foot" (Matt. 5:13). Unfortunately, it does not appear historically that the saltiness of a passionate faith was ever restored in Sardis. Ramsay writes that "Sardis today is a wilderness of ruins and thorns, pastures and wild-flowers, where the only habitations are a few huts of Yuruk nomads beside the temple of Cybele in the low ground by the Pactolus, and at the distance of a mile two modern houses by the railway station."[16] There are many churches in North America that are in danger of becoming a vacant reminder of better days. For the people of God, the best days are always ahead, not because of who we are, but because of the God who calls us into his future.

Questions for Group Discussion

1. In what ways is the church today experiencing "ecclesiastical sleepwalking"?
2. Which of the five imperatives given by the Revelator speaks to you?
3. Which of Reggie McNeal's questions is the most relevant to your church context?

6

Philadelphia

The Spirit of Fear

"And to the angel of the church in Philadelphia write:
. . . Look, I have set before you an open door, which no
one is able to shut. I know that you have but little power,
and yet you have kept my word and have not denied my
name. . . . If you conquer, I will make you a pillar in the
temple of my God."

It was Friday, June 28, 1991, at exactly 7:48 am. Debbie and I had
recently moved to Pasadena so that I could attend Fuller Theological Seminary, and we were living in an upper-floor apartment in
student housing. The alarm clock had just rung at 7:45, and I was
sitting on the edge of the bed preparing to head for the shower when
suddenly everything began to move. For a split second I thought that
it might just be someone rolling a cart or stroller outside on the deck,
because whenever anyone walked past our apartment things shook a
bit. But this was much more than a passing stroller; everything was

103

moving. It took me only a moment to realize that we were having an earthquake.

Being new to Southern California, I did not know much about what to do during a quake. I know now that we were already in the safest place a person can be during an earthquake—bed—but somewhere in my mind I seemed to remember that a doorframe is the right place to stand and ride out the quake. So leaping up, I grabbed Debbie by the arm and pulled her into the doorway of our bedroom.

The next few seconds were quite surreal. Pictures were falling off the wall and almost everything sitting on tables or counters leapt to the floor. Many of the kitchen cabinets opened up and many of our newlywed dishes danced out. Strangest of all was watching our small refrigerator hop from its place to the center of the kitchen floor, discarding much of its contents along the way.

Although it seemed like much longer, the quake was over in just a matter of moments. We had just experienced a 5.8 magnitude earthquake centered a few miles east of us in the small town of Sierra Madre. On the one hand, our first SoCal quake was quite traumatic. Not only did we lose a few possessions, but we were also psychologically on edge for the next few days as we experienced several aftershocks and watched one sensationalized news report after another predicting the "big one" in the not-too-distant future. Just a couple of days after the quake, I was studying in the seminary lounge when I felt a small thud and heard a slight rumble. I instinctively ducked underneath the table where I was studying. I would have felt really stupid had another student not been under the table with me. We laughed together when we realized that we had just ducked for cover from the air conditioning.

But my most vivid memory of the June 28 earthquake was what took place the rest of that Friday. Living in an apartment complex full of students, everyone immediately began checking on one another. Those of us living on the second floor seemed to have experienced the most damage, and so apartment by apartment we helped one another clean up. Since classes were canceled for the day and structures were checked for damage, a couple of colleagues and I got on our bicycles and began to ride around town to see what kind of damage had taken place.

Pasadena is typical of most places that are part of a big city. People who live in large cities like Los Angeles tend to be deeply shaped by a basic fear of "the other." Most of the time people don't look one another in the eye as they walk down the street. In public, some part of you is always on guard against what someone else might do to you. But on this day it seemed that all the barriers between neighbors had been taken down.

Some of the barriers had literally collapsed, as fences, walls, and a few chimneys had fallen over. But as we rode around the neighborhood and started helping people clean up, we found that those conditioned to avoid one another were giving one another a needed hand. People were staying home from work and were outside because everyone was checking on the condition of their homes, but they were also helping one another. I will never forget how such a frightening day also became one of the most profound experiences of neighbor-love that I have ever experienced, especially in an urban context. That day, people who usually don't look one another in the eye became friends. A day that began in fear ended in community.

Philadelphia: The Missionary City

The city of Philadelphia was not an ancient city. It had been founded by Attalus II in 140 BCE. Attalus also bore the name Philadelphos, and thus the new city was named after its founder. Philadelphia stood in a strategic location on the border of the countries of Mysia, Lydia, and Phrygia. Because of its prime location, it had been established by Attalus as a missionary city of sorts. The small city was founded for the purpose of consolidating and educating the central regions of Asia. The mission of Philadelphia was to bring Hellenism—or Greek culture—to the recently annexed areas of Lydia and Phrygia, and it was highly successful in its mission. Although the dominant language of the area had been Lydian, by the first century the dominant language, with the help of Philadelphia, was Greek.

Philadelphia enjoyed considerable prosperity by capitalizing on an economy based on agriculture and industry. It also became a major center for temple worship and religious festivals. Apparently there was a large and influential Jewish population there, and by the fifth century CE Philadelphia had come to be known as "little Athens" for its many temples devoted in particular to Dionysus.[1]

The one major drawback as a city was its tendency to experience earthquakes. Philadelphia was located on the edge of a highly active volcanic area that blessed the city with rich, fertile soil and curative hot springs but also provided it with frequent tremors and jolts from periodic earthquakes. Johnson writes that "whenever a quake struck, the people of Philadelphia would flee the city. When the aftershocks subsided they would return. The people of Philadelphia were, therefore, 'always going out and coming in; they were always fleeing the city and returning to it.'"[2]

In 17 CE, a devastating earthquake leveled twelve Asian cities in the Lydian valley (including Sardis) and was particularly severe in Philadelphia. The quake nearly destroyed the city, leaving the people in a heightened sense of angst because of the high number of aftershocks they experienced. The city was thus shaped by a spirit of fear that lasted for a number of years. Even three years later, in 20 CE, many inhabitants remained outside the city living in huts and booths. Those who stayed in Philadelphia tried several methods to rebuild the walls of the city and their homes to protect them from the recurring shocks. Ramsay states that "the memory of this disaster lived long. . . . [The] people lived amid ever threatening danger, in dread always of a new disaster; and the habit of going out to the open country had probably not disappeared when the Seven Letters were written."[3]

As we will see in the letter itself, of the seven churches addressed by the Revelator, Philadelphia is most praised. This is certainly the church that the one who speaks through the Revelator loves. It is likely that the context of the apocalyptic language contained in this letter is closely related to the fear that remained in Philadelphia after the great earthquake of 17 BCE.

Four Major Challenges

It is apparent from both history and the letter of the Revelator that the church in Philadelphia faced several obstacles. The first obstacle was that they had apparently been shut out of synagogue worship. John not only makes reference twice to a "door which no one is able to shut" (Rev. 3:7–8) but also references "those of the synagogue of Satan who say that they are Jews and are not" (3:9). Claiming to be the sole possessors of "the key of David," the Jewish population in Philadelphia was apparently excluding the Christians in the city from participation in the synagogue. The door of worship and fellowship had been shut to the Christians.

It was not unusual in the first century for Jews and Christians to come into conflict. These conflicts were primarily theological in nature. Christians claimed to be the heirs of the sacred Hebrew history and to be worshiping the one who was the fulfillment of the Jewish messianic expectations. That the Christians included gentiles, many if not most of whom did not follow the covenantal laws of circumcision and dietary restriction, certainly compounded the conflict. Inevitable conflict arose over who were the "real Jews." The Revelator writes to Philadelphia about those who "say that they are Jews and are not" (3:9), thereby seeming to side not with those who are Jews by birth but those—like the Christians of Philadelphia—who are now Jews by faith. As Mounce writes, "It was the church that could now be called 'the Israel of God' (Gal. 6:16), for the Jewish nation had forfeited that privilege by disbelief. Members of the local synagogue may claim to be Jews, but the very claim constitutes them liars."[4]

It is also quite likely that the Christians in Philadelphia were facing persecution because of their exclusion from the synagogue. It was often the case that as long as the followers of Jesus were perceived as another sect within Judaism, they were afforded the protections granted to the Jews. For example, as long as the Jews continued to pay taxes, they were excluded from forced participation in the imperial cult. But if the Christian church was excluded from the worship practices of the Jewish faith, they were no longer subject to its protections. It is quite possible that the Jews in Philadelphia not only strongly disliked the believers but also feared that the inclusion of gentiles in the church might jeopardize their protected status with the authorities. Thus the Jews in Philadelphia were apparently aggressive in their hostility toward the church and claimed that they—Israel—alone had access to the door of God's kingdom.

The church in Philadelphia also faced an issue of power. John acknowledges that the church had "but little power" (Rev. 3:8), which suggests that it probably had few members and was poor in resources. Although they were in the eyes of the world weak in financial wherewithal and political significance, they were nevertheless honored by the Lord because they "have kept my word and have not denied my name" (3:8).

The church also faced the challenge of being scattered due to the continual fear of disaster. As I pointed out earlier, many of the citizens had left the city after the earthquake of 17 BCE due to fear of the city's complete collapse. So although people came to do business in the city, many had moved outside its walls to escape the risk of physical catastrophe.

Finally, the church of Philadelphia also faced the obstacle of living in a city that had been deeply shaped by the power and influence of the Roman Empire. During the rebuilding of the city after the earthquake, Philadelphia took on a new name—*Neocaesarea*, the city of the Young Caesar. This new name was most likely a special gift granted to the city by Tiberius, thus consecrating it to the service and worship of the empire. The city and its emperor entered into a kind of covenant. In exchange for financial assistance and the help of the empire to rebuild the city, Philadelphia and its citizens devoted the city to the honor of its divine benefactor. Taking on the name of caesar was probably regarded as a wise political move and a highly honorable practice. As a consequence, the city and the emperor were tightly bound to each other.

This unique relationship could have only exacerbated the fears of the Philadelphian church. Excluded from the protection of the synagogue, the Christians certainly faced persecution for not fully participating in the cultic worship of Tiberius. It is probably because the city had written on itself the name of the imperial god—caesar— who had come to its aid after the disaster, that John encourages the Philadelphian church, "I will write on you the name of my God" (3:12). In keeping with the overall theme of the entire Revelation, John encourages the church in Philadelphia to be strong "in the hour of trial that is coming" (3:10). John reminds the believers that they are not alone in facing such trials but that when the Lord of the churches returns, the hour of trial will be "coming on the whole world to test the inhabitants of the earth" (3:10).

Faustian bargains like the one made between the city and the empire last only so long. Ramsay argues that by the time the seven letters were written, the shrine to the emperor was most likely in a state of dilapidation and decay. "Accordingly there would be an opening for a telling contrast, such as St. John so frequently aims at, between the shifting facts of ordinary city life and the more permanent character of the analogous institutions and promises of the Divine Author."[5]

The Philadelphians were left with a run-down temple and obsolete worship practices developed during a time when they had needed the deliverance of the powers that be. Although they had been proud to bear the name of the one who delivered them in their time of distress, that deliverance had not been permanent, and there remained for them "nothing of which the city could now feel proud."[6] In contrast, the Lord was promising eternal benefits to those who remained faithful. He promises to make the people "a pillar in the temple of my God; you will never go out of it. I will write on you the name of my God, and the name of the city of my God, the new Jerusalem that comes down from my God out of heaven, and my own new name" (3:12).

Tiberius had claimed the city of Philadelphia as his own, and the city was subsequently neglected. Christ has claimed the church of Philadelphia, and thus it will bear a crown and a name that will never be removed (3:11).

An Open Door

How does a church that faces these many obstacles become the church Christ loves? Most commentators believe that the key to understanding the goodness of the Philadelphian church is found in the Revelator's use of the term "open door." "Look," writes John, "I have set before you an open door, which no one is able to shut" (3:8). It is unlikely that this open door refers to the possibility of the Christians returning to the synagogue from which they have been excluded. Rather, it is much more likely that this term is a Pauline metaphor that passed into ordinary usage in the early church. This term carried with it a double meaning.

Christ had given to the church in Philadelphia an open door of relationship with himself. In the Gospel of John, Jesus declares that he, the shepherd, is himself the door (John 10:7, 9). Even if the door of the synagogue is closed to them, the doorway to the Father—Jesus himself—will never be closed. As Koester writes, "This assures them that even though their adversaries seek to exclude them, Christ has opened the way into the presence of God for them. In the eyes of society they may be outsiders, but through Christ they are insiders."[7]

This "open door" is also a clear reference to the opportunity for evangelism. In 1 Corinthians 16:9 Paul writes that a "wide door for effective work has opened to me." Likewise in 2 Corinthians 2:12 he states, "When I came to Troas . . . a door was opened for me in the Lord." Also, in Colossians 4:3 Paul encourages the believers there to "Pray for us . . . that God will open to us a door for the word." In each of these passages the term "door" or "open door" is used to describe a unique door of opportunity, especially an opportunity for mission activity. It appears that Philadelphia became the "beloved" church because they turned their various challenges into open doors for evangelism. Concerning this Johnson writes:

> Here is where we really see the brilliance of Jesus. Philadelphia was founded in 140 B.C. for one over-riding purpose: to be a base from which to launch a campaign to Hellenize the world—to be a base from which to spread the Greek language, worldview and way of life to the whole world. . . . A missionary city for everything Greek! From now on the city would be a base for launching a new campaign, the campaign to gospelize the world.[8]

I am convinced that this is the reason Christ so deeply loved the church in Philadelphia. This was a church in which obstacles became opportunities. This ability to overcome a spirit of fear is the unique gift of the Philadelphian church, because there is nothing similar mentioned about any of the other six cities.

I have this crazy imagination about the church in Philadelphia. I imagine that rather than shrinking after being shut out of the synagogue, the church leaders gathered together and figured out how they could begin to meet wherever they might find space to set apart for worship. If the synagogue is shut, then it opens all the other doors.

When the church realizes that it doesn't have enough resources, it doesn't focus on what it does not possess but rather sees its limited resources as an opportunity for God to bestow blessings and provision on them from his unlimited resources. I believe that the Christians in Philadelphia did not see the surrounding culture of fear as a problem but as an opportunity to speak to people about where real security can be found. Instead of seeing the scattered community of Philadelphia as a problem, my guess is that the spirit of the community allowed the church to go out into the byways where the people were living instead of wishing they could return to the centrality of the city. The spirit of the Philadelphian Christians viewed the radical covenant the city had made with the empire not as an insurmountable problem but as an opportunity for believers to be radically different.

This was the spirit of the Philadelphian church. It was a church that moved beyond a spirit of fear and allowed its obstacles to become, through the power of Christ, open doors of opportunity for building the kingdom and extending the gospel.

Problems and Possibilities

The modern church also faces all kinds of obstacles and transitions. It seems increasingly obvious to those involved in church leadership that on a variety of levels things are rapidly changing. Terms such as "postmodernism" are used to try to describe the sweeping transitions that are taking place culturally, politically, economically, technologically, and philosophically. All of these changes are having a deep impact on the church.

There are many who argue that, although the church is always reforming in some way, we are on the cusp of another major period of reformation. The Protestant Reformation brought not only vast theological changes to the medieval church but also totally different worship practices and political structures. Before the Reformation, it would have been nearly impossible for believers to predict that a new theological perspective combined with the rise of the nation-state and the opportunity for every believer to read the Bible in his or her own language would give to Christianity the multitude of denominations we have today.

When the Reformation took place, there were two very different reactions. Some moved forward cautiously and optimistically, believing that God was moving in a new and fresh way; others, in a spirit of fear, retrenched even deeper in the culture of medieval Christian faith and practice.

There is no question that we are again in a time of sweeping change. The massive changes in technology, communication, and the exchange of information go without saying and are having a huge impact on the church. But it would seem that there are cultural and philosophical transitions going on of which we are just beginning to become aware. Although religious faith has been kept separate from the operation of the state in North America, the American church has nevertheless been profoundly shaped by the older nation-state religious model. When we meet, where we meet, the benefits we receive from the state, and the way that many sacred institutions (such as marriage) have been adopted as civil institutions are just a few examples of the sticky relationship of influence the church and state have had on each other, even while remaining ideologically separate.

Living as we do in an increasingly multicultural, multireligious, and secularized state, we should not be surprised that the patterns and structures of the post-Reformation state church are also in transition. When the church meets, where the church meets, what the church does when it meets, who leads the church meeting, and what name the church meets under are all questions that are currently in flux. In the midst of these changes the church also feels as though it has lost its power in the culture wars, and its people feel increasingly irrelevant and marginalized in the political dialogue.

Given the sweeping cultural changes, we too, like the church in Philadelphia and the post-Reformation church, will have the choice to retrench in a spirit of fear or view these challenges—as the Philadelphians did—as open doors and opportunities for God to move in new and unique ways. Certainly several books could, and routinely do, address the challenges the modern church faces and how we should face them, but let me mention three major obstacles—or opportunities—that the church faces today. These obstacles can become either moments in which the church is captured by the deadly spirit of fear or moments for moving forward by God's grace.

One of the unique challenges facing the American church is the increasing ethnic and cultural diversity of the population. In North America the growth rate of Caucasians is 0 percent, while the African-American, Hispanic, and Asian populations in the country are experiencing double-digit expansion. By 2050, only half of America's population will be Caucasian.[9]

There are many in the church who find the increasing diversity of the culture to be an insurmountable threat to the growth and vitality of the church. It is painful to confess that the church in North America remains the nation's most segregated institution. I serve on a board of church administration that unfortunately continues to have to close churches that have failed to find ways to integrate with the changing demographics of their surrounding neighborhoods. Thankfully there are new models and new voices arising in the church world that are calling believers to diversity, not only because it is a pragmatic method for survival, but also because it is an amazing opportunity to truly become the Pentecostal church—in the truest sense of the word—that God has called us to be. It does not take the Spirit of God to create a homogenous group of people—such groups are called country clubs. I don't believe that it is even fully necessary to have the Spirit of God help create a mono-generational congregation. For several years I worked as a pastor to college-age students. I often tell people that it isn't that hard to build a college group. You just offer free food and (to borrow a line from John Ortberg) speak on three topics: sex, the end times, and sex in the end times.

Uniformity of race, class, age, and so on can be established without God's divine power. Unity in diversity is an open door of opportunity for the Spirit to build a unique community that witnesses to the power of God's reconciling grace in the world. The deadly spirit of fear too often captures the church and keeps it from moving toward "the other," but thankfully there are church leaders and models for ministry that are rising up to call the church to walk through the open door of diversity.[10]

Another important challenge facing the church is the increasing separation between the rich and the poor. No nation on earth has a greater net worth than the United States, but that wealth is distributed unequally. Forty percent of the nation's assets are held by 1 percent of the population. Thirty million Americans live in poverty. Forty percent of those in poverty are children.[11] Like its approach to ethnic diversity, the church often runs from the increasing economic challenges that the culture faces. For every dollar spent on ministry to the poor, the average American church spends more than five dollars on buildings and maintenance.

Finally, the family as an institution is in decline. One out of every four marriages in the United States will end in divorce. Cohabitation has risen by more than 500 percent in the last two decades (even though people who cohabitate prior to marriage have an 82 percent greater chance of divorce than couples who marry without having lived together first). One out of every three children born this year will be born to an unwed mother. The church is not immune from these influences. The divorce rate among people who call themselves "born-again" Christians is 27 percent and among non-believers it is 24 percent.[12]

I could go on and talk about the influence of the media on the millennial generation. For example, it is believed that children of the millennial generation will have an attention span of approximately six minutes. The illiteracy rate is beginning to climb culturally, and the rate of biblical illiteracy is the highest it has ever been in United States history.

All of these changes and dozens more pose serious challenges to the way the church works and lives in the world. The question the church must continually ask itself is, do we see these changing realities as obstacles to the gospel or opportunities for God's transforming work in the world? Philadelphia was praised because it refused to allow itself to be possessed by a spirit of fear but instead turned its obstacles into open doors for the building of the kingdom.

Philadelphia in History

Long after all of the country of Philadelphia had fallen into the hands of the Turks, the church of Philadelphia remained. Through the fourteenth century CE, Philadelphia stood nearly alone in the midst of a Turkish land. It became the longest existing church of any of the seven churches of Revelation. What gave the church its staying power? I am convinced that it had the spirit to name its challenges and to see those challenges as opportunities.

William Barclay writes that Philadelphia had a lovely custom regarding the construction of its temples. When a person had served the state well—when he left behind a noble record as a magistrate or as a benefactor to the city or as a priest—"the memorial which the city gave to him was to erect a pillar in one of the temples with his name inscribed upon it."[13] These pillars served not only as memorials but also as supports on which a new temple was established.

In this letter to the church in Philadelphia, Christ promises to make the faithful of the church into pillars inscribed with the very name of God. These pillars serve both as a memorial to the work of God and as supports for the new temple that God is building through them. I believe that Christ is still looking to establish pillars inscribed with his name to use in the building of his new temple. There is no question that we are in a culture of radical change, a culture that poses all kinds of obstacles to the faith, but with God's help we can overcome the spirit of fear and become pillars of faith that will support the new work that God is doing among us.

Questions for Group Discussion

1. What was the spirit of the church in Philadelphia that made it so honored by the Lord of the churches?
2. What fears do you sense in the church?
3. How might the church conquer the often deadly spirit of fear?

7

Laodicea

The Spirit of Self-Sufficiency

"And to the angel of the church in Laodicea write: . . .
I wish that you were either cold or hot. So, because you
are lukewarm, and neither cold nor hot, I am about to
spit you out of my mouth. For you say, 'I am rich, I have
prospered, and I need nothing.'"

grew up in a denomination that in its early days had its share of
folks who would start jumping and shouting when they got blessed
in a worship service. Although most of the churches in my tradition
are fairly reserved and refined today, there was a time when people
responded to the presence of the Holy Spirit with all sorts of bodily
reactions, including running. There is one particular "blessed" story
that my family loves to tell. My grandfather was the pastor of a large
church in Oklahoma when they built a grand and beautiful sanctuary
that would seat between two thousand five hundred and three thousand people. There was a gentleman in the congregation who would

frequently get blessed, stand up, and start shouting while running a complete lap around the congregation. People had grown used to this brother's expressiveness and his frequent Sunday lap around the old, and significantly smaller, sanctuary. However, on the first Sunday in the new sanctuary, the brother got blessed and took off for his first lap around three thousand seats. The lap began with running and ended with dragging. It began with shouting but ended with panting. Most importantly, it started during the congregational singing but ended at the time set aside for pastoral prayer. The previously charged-up brother's return to his seat was perfectly synched with my grandfather's step forward into the pulpit to lead the time of prayer. As the gentleman panted back to his seat to collapse, my grandfather simply looked down and said, "It's a lot farther around this one isn't it, brother?"

Without question the most familiar of the seven letters is the one to the church in Laodicea. The image of lukewarm water being spewed from the mouth of the Lord is a graphic word picture that has deeply captured the imagination of the church for generations. I have usually associated the lukewarm spirituality of Laodicea with a Christian faith devoid of passion. Often a "hot" faith is linked to the intensity of worship expression or an intense desire to share one's faith with others. This text has been used again and again to make people who don't raise their hands when they sing or don't go door-to-door handing out evangelistic tracts feel guilty for their lukewarm spirituality. Although there is certainly a place for getting past one's self-consciousness in worship and for having a desire to share one's Christian faith with others, the lukewarmness of Laodicea is much more prevalent in the church than simply a lack of expressiveness and much more deadly than evangelism without megaphones. The lukewarmness of Laodicea was caused by the spirit of self-sufficiency that says, "I am rich, I have prospered, and I need nothing."

Laodicea: The Prosperous City

Laodicea, the last of the cities visited by John's messenger and the last addressed in the Asian letters, was a very wealthy city. The city was built as a fortress situated at the convergence of three major roads.

Scholars often find Laodicea difficult to describe because it had "no extremes, and hardly any very strong marked features."[1] Its security, balance, and ability to compromise for the sake of peace aided its development and its prosperity.

It is speculated that the church of Laodicea was most likely founded on Paul's third missionary journey while he spent time at Ephesus (Acts 19:10), perhaps by Epaphras (Col. 4:12).[2] There is no evidence that Paul ever visited the church, although he apparently wrote them a letter that is now lost (4:16). Like the city itself, the church in Laodicea was obviously quite wealthy and secure. Like the letter to Sardis, what is not included is highly instructive. There is no mention of persecution, of trouble with the Jewish population, or any conflict with heresy. Although there were some in Sardis who were considered faithful, there are no believers who are praised in this letter. Rather, all stand equally condemned by the Revelator. Ladd believes that "it is probably that many of the church members were active participants in the affluent society, and that the very economic affluence had exercised a deadly influence on the spiritual life of the church."[3] This affluence was due to the economy of Laodicea, which was founded on three areas: banking, clothing, and its medical school.

Because it was situated at the convergence of three roads, Laodicea was the center of banking for Asia Minor. Its financial prosperity was demonstrated when, after suffering damage from a severe earthquake in 60 CE, it refused imperial help and financed its own rebuilding effort. Tacitus, the Roman historian, writes that Laodicea "arose from the ruins by the strength of her own resources, and with no help from us."[4] In 100 CE, just a few years after the Revelator wrote this letter, another earthquake nearly destroyed the city, and again it financed its own restoration without imperial aid.

Laodicea was also famous for manufacturing black woolen cloth used for clothing and carpets. Fine and expensive garments from Laodicea were exported all over the known world. "The Laodiceans were the best-dressed people of the Roman province of Asia."[5]

There was also a flourishing medical school in Laodicea that was especially famous for its eye salve. Located on the border of Phrygia, the pharmacists of Laodicea had discovered how to use "Phrygian powder" to make a salve that was believed to heal weak and failing eyes.

Biblical scholars believe there is an important link between the prosperity of the city and the spiritual failing of the Laodicean church (see Rev. 3:17), and Ladd sees a specific link between Laodicea's spiritual complacency and its spiritual pride. He writes concerning Laodicea, "No doubt part of her problem was the inability to distinguish between material and spiritual prosperity. The church that is prospering materially and outwardly can easily fall into the self-deception that her outward prosperity is the measure of her spiritual prosperity."[6] French sociologist Jacques Ellul argues that it is the goal of every urban civilization to ultimately make God irrelevant and unnecessary. "The whole goal of the 'city of man,'" writes Ellul, "is to be able to say, 'We did it ourselves, we did it our way, we made it on our own, we have need of nothing.'"[7] Unfortunately it is this spirit of self-sufficiency that separates Laodicea from the life-giving source of its savior.

Disconnected from the Source of Life

For all of Laodicea's economic advantages, its one outstanding shortcoming was its poor water supply. A few miles to the southeast of Laodicea was the city of Colossae, which was famous for its cool mineral springs. To the north was Hierapolis, a city famous for its hot medicinal waters, which attracted hundreds of visitors each year seeking cures for various ailments. The water supply for Laodicea was piped to the city through an aqueduct from springs about six miles to the south. There were obvious disadvantages to receiving its water supply in this manner. The city was vulnerable to any enemy that might cut off its supply, and the water was warm by the time it arrived in the city through the maze of clay irrigation pipes. The distance of the city from its supply of life-giving water made it weak and its water undesirable. Further, lukewarm water was used as an agent to induce vomiting.

Given this state of affairs, perhaps it is best to understand the lukewarmness of the Laodicean church not as some form of unexpressive spirituality but as a spirit of self-sufficiency that in reality is distant and cut off from its primary source of life, namely, Christ. In essence the Revelator is contrasting the hot medicinal waters of Hierapolis and the cold, refreshing waters of Colossae. The spirituality of the church in Laodicea was neither healing nor life giving. It was instead completely ineffective in its self-sufficiency.

Like so much of Revelation, when the material realm is viewed through the interpretive lenses of God's reign, reality is brought into a new light. In this letter to Laodicea the reader can see the unique spiritual insight of the Revelator again at work. John continually holds up a lens to that which seems appealing and healthy and allows the reader to see the true nature of what is being perceived. Like the goddess Roma—who appears to hold the cup of life, but when viewed through the enlightened eyes of Revelation is revealed as the whore of Babylon who extends to those who partake in her life the cup of death—the church of Laodicea may appear affluent, healthy, and in need of nothing. But from the perspective of the Revelator, this church is "wretched, pitiable, poor, blind, and naked" (3:17). It is interesting that these words of condemnation from the Lord take those things of which the Laodiceans are most proud and turn them upside-down. The wealthy and powerful banking center of Asia is in reality "wretched, pitiable, and poor" in its faith. The city famous for its fine fabrics and expensive clothes is really morally "naked" before the Lord. And the place known far and wide for its healing eye salve is in reality spiritually "blind."

The pretentious claim of the Laodiceans has been unmasked and revealed for what it truly is: the weakness of the spirit of self-sufficiency. Now that they have been revealed as poor and spiritually ineffective, the Lord of the churches calls the Laodicean believers to "buy from me gold refined by fire so that you may be rich; and white robes to clothe you and to keep the shame of your nakedness from being seen; and salve to anoint your eyes so that you may see" (3:18).

Material Prosperity and the Spirit of Self-Sufficiency

I am sure that it does not have to be this way, but more often than not there appears to be an important link between spiritual complacency and material blessing. The church that is prospering financially and numerically can easily slip into the self-deception that its outward prosperity is also a measure of its spiritual health. John Wesley was often concerned about the effect of riches and success on the nature of faith. Wesley wrote in 1786:

> I fear, wherever riches have increased, the essence of religion has decreased in the same proportion. Therefore, I do not see how it is possible, in the nature of things, for any revival of religion to continue long. For religion must necessarily produce both industry and frugality, and these cannot but produce riches. But as riches increase, so will pride, anger, and love of the world in all its branches.[8]

I wish this was not the case, but I fear that Wesley is right. I want to be very clear and careful here. There are times that I find myself in dialogue with religious leaders, theological scholars, and church practitioners and a particular size of attendance and income is held up as "the model" for what a church should be. I may be overly sensitive on this point because as the pastor of a large congregation I sense—especially among scholars—that small churches are held up as the model for the "true church" and large congregations are viewed as religious corporations catering to the Christian consumer. Personally, I think there are incredible benefits, as well as incredible dangers, in both small and large churches. A small church is not always a holier church filled with more spiritually mature people, and a large church is not always a consumer organization filled with nominal believers. Sometimes smaller is just smaller, but certainly critical to our reading of the letter to the church in Laodicea is getting past the bias that bigger and richer is always better. For Laodicea, material strength was not a sign of spiritual blessing; it was a temptation to become self-sufficient.

Although I am sure the spirit of self-sufficiency makes its appearance in several forms in the modern church, let me point out just one example and use a familiar Old Testament story to narrate the problem. One way that the deadly spirit of self-sufficiency makes its appearance in the modern church is through the cult of personality. In a media-savvy, image-obsessed culture like our own, the famous prophetic words of Marshall McLuhan—"The medium is the message"—are often fulfilled. Media scholar Neil Postman frequently pointed out that in a television age many former presidents, including Franklin D. Roosevelt, would most likely not be able to get elected because, although their ideas were expressed well in a print or radio age, their image would not have met the demands of a visual age. The church in America has certainly reaped an abundance of blessings and curses with the onset of the television age, and the Internet age only seems to be upping the ante. I am very thankful for the instant availability of electronic resources today for those who are growing in the faith, but at the same time I am personally and painfully aware of the tension churches feel trying to match substance with style.

I recently had the opportunity to hear a speaker who has become somewhat of a celebrity du jour in Christian circles. I was excited to hear this particular person speak, and I was very pleased with what the person had to say, but it was clear from the sets in the background, the images on the screen, the person's wardrobe, and even the hairstyle that media consultants had been hard at work making sure that every image resonated with the target audience.

Again, I want to be very careful here because I know personally not only the pressure of trying to communicate the gospel to a media-savvy generation but also the inner pressure of wanting to give God our very best in whatever we do. My concern, however—at least in this chapter—is not for those who find that they cannot compete in a church culture that has been captured by the cult of personality (I have a different set of concerns for those who unfortunately feel alienated or marginalized in the present culture). My concern is for those who are able to succeed in a church culture obsessed with personality because those leaders and the churches they lead are extremely vulnerable to the spirit of self-sufficiency. Gifted, attractive, intelligent, and creative leaders need God's Spirit, but they are also fully capable of succeeding without him.

Even a cursory reading of the Old Testament reminds us that it has always been God's tendency to choose those who are not strong or mighty in the eyes of the world to be the instruments of his revelation in the world. There are so many narratives that I could choose from to make this point, but certainly my favorite is the anointing of David in 1 Samuel 16. Here the Lord leads Samuel the prophet to the house of Jesse to anoint the future successor to Saul's throne. Eliab, the eldest son, enters Samuel's presence first. When Samuel sees Eliab, he thinks, "Surely the LORD's anointed is now before the LORD." But the Lord replies to Samuel with those words that we hold to be so important: "Do not look on his appearance or on the height of his stature, because I have rejected him; for the LORD does not see as mortals see; they look on the outward appearance, but the LORD looks on the heart" (1 Sam. 16:7).

Certainly this verse is an important reminder that the qualifications for being of service to God are not based on externals, but my favorite part of this narrative is the Hebrew word Jesse uses to describe his missing son when Samuel asks, "Are all your sons here?" Jesse replies to Samuel, "There remains yet the youngest, but he is keeping the sheep" (16:11). The Hebrew word translated here as "youngest" is the word *haqqaton* (pronounced "hawk-a-ton"). The word *haqqaton* can literally be translated as "the runt of the litter." Thus Jesse is essentially saying, "There remains the runt of the litter, but I'm not sure that you really want to see him. We have given him the job that doesn't take a lot of ability, the job for the kid who didn't do so well on the standardized tests. He's out keeping the sheep."

There are many reasons why I like the word *haqqaton*. I like that one really has to spit to say it correctly. I love that the greatest king in Israel's history was essentially overlooked by his family but not by God. But I especially love that God seems to always pick *haqqatons* to be his messengers. I have preached often on David the *haqqaton*. It is a word that we use around our house with some frequency— and we use it well. "Get out of my chair you little *haqqaton*," for instance. On the Sunday that I was installed as pastor of my current church, the denominational leader who was installing me told the congregation, "I informed the church board when we began the search process that our journey would be much like Samuel's as he went to anoint a new king. Like Eliab and his brothers who passed before Samuel, several gifted candidates for senior pastor came across the desk. But none of them were God's chosen person . . ." He continued by describing me as the one God had chosen for this church at this time, but it was too late. My wife and two oldest children had heard all my sermons and knew the story of David too well, and thus they were beside themselves cracking up as they sat on the front row. On one of the most significant days of my career, I was being called a *haqqaton* in front of everyone, and they knew it. I saw my family laughing and I couldn't help it; I started giggling also. The church · official leading the ceremony is a friend, and I know he was trying to give me a compliment, but all I heard was God confirming what I already knew to be true: I have no external qualifications for the task to which I have been called.

In a church culture shaped by the cult of personality, every church leader needs to be reminded that he or she is a *haqqaton*. Apart from a connection to the power of Christ and a reliance on his Spirit, our work for the kingdom is in vain. There are certainly many other ways that the spirit of self-reliance finds its way into the modern church. It is easy for churches to become dependent on flashy programs, gifted musicians, or elaborate facilities as a way to build the church. Again, I do not wish to be misunderstood. Meaningful programs, powerful worship, and facilities that form a sacred space for people to encounter God have their place in the life and ministry of the church, but if we are not careful we can become like Laodicea and build for ourselves a great economy while cutting ourselves off from the life-giving presence of the Lord.

Opening the Door

Revelation 3:20 is perhaps the most quoted verse in all of Revelation. "Listen! I am standing at the door, knocking; if you hear my voice and open the door, I will come in to you and eat with you, and you with me." This verse has been immortalized in the famous painting of Jesus knocking at the door and is often used as an evangelistic call for people to open the doors of their hearts to invite Jesus in as Lord and savior. Although this is certainly not an inappropriate way to interpret this verse, it is interesting to note that this statement by Jesus is given within the context of a church—Laodicea—and the reference to eating probably has to do with participation in the Lord's Supper. The call to open the door, in this context, is not made to the nonbeliever or to a group of nonbelievers. The call to open the door is made to the church, to the followers of Christ themselves! In their self-sufficiency, the church of Laodicea has in some way made Christ an outsider to the congregation that bears his name. In the central act of the church's worship—in Laodicea's case it was the act of Eucharist—Christ has been left outside knocking at the door. When the church begins to live off its prosperity, its comfort, and its self-sufficiency, we get programs without spiritual power, preaching without prophetic revelation, prayer without divine presence, and church membership without missional living.

The letter to Laodicea is in some ways the harshest of the seven letters, but it is also full of hope. The Lord reproves and disciplines those whom he loves (3:19). Christ is summoning the members of a lukewarm and complacent church back to spiritual vitality and passion. Even though the church has inadvertently cut itself off from connection to the true vine, Christ still stands at the door seeking to dine with his children.

The church of Laodicea, possessed by the spirit of self-sufficiency, had the opportunity to repent. Opening the door to the presence of Christ would have to begin with confessing their deep need for his presence. The church cannot rely on its wealth and prestige to bring about its redemption; rather, it must receive from the Lord his gold refined by fire. The church cannot depend on its expensive garments to cover its vulnerability and nakedness; it must instead purify its life and receive the white robes of new life that come only from the hand of God. The church cannot receive healing for its blindness from its famous salve; it must receive spiritual discernment and vision from the healing hand of Christ.

One last time we are exhorted by the Lord of the church to "listen to what the Spirit is saying to the churches" (3:22). The letters addressed to the seven churches are a collective word to the universal church throughout time. The seven deadly spirits that captured the churches of Asia Minor are still at work in today's church. I turn now to some final words on how as leaders we can, by the power of God, redeem the angels of the churches.

Questions for Group Discussion

1. Why is there so often a link between prosperity and self-sufficient faith?
2. In what ways has the church at times cut itself off from the source of its life—Jesus Christ?
3. What does the lesson of the *haqqaton* remind us about God's activity?

8

The Ears to Hear

A student once answered a cell phone in the middle of a class I was teaching and, loud enough for all in the class to hear, said, "Hello. . . . I'm in Church History Class. . . . It's fine. . . . There's not much of a point to it, but it's okay. . . . I'd better go. Everyone is looking at me." I'm not sure what question elicited the response, "There's not much of a point to it," but I've always hoped the question was perhaps, "Why are you in school?" But I'm afraid the question was most likely, "Is it a good class?"

It might be good at the conclusion to this study of the seven letters in Revelation to ask the question, "What's the point?" Is the point of studying these seven letters simply to look at the spirit of churches such as Sardis or Laodicea and compare their angels with the ethos or spirit of our own homes, communities, and churches, or is there something deeper going on? I believe that more than seeing something of ourselves in one of the deadly spirits, the point of the seven letters is the transformation of the church into a community that rightly bears the name "the body of Christ." The Lord of the church concludes the letters by inviting "anyone who has an ear [to] listen to what the Spirit is saying to the churches" (Rev. 3:22), which

leads me to wonder, how do we learn to hear what the Spirit is saying to the churches? Are there patterns we can discover that will help
those of us who are called to lead the church to discern the deadly
spirits? And after discerning the spirit of the church, how do we work
to transform a deadly spirit to a life-giving one?

I have struggled greatly to begin answering these questions in
my own ministry. The more familiar I have become with the letters
to the churches in Revelation, the more convinced I am that what
John is doing is more an art than a science. Although it is my nature
to shy away from creating simplistic "step one, step two, and step
three" spiritual formulas (especially if they all start with the same
letter) because life doesn't seem to fit in neat three-point packages,
I do believe that a pattern for transformation emerges within each
of the letters to the churches. I believe that transformation of the
deadly spirits begins when we are able to name the spirit of the
church, call that spirit to repentance, and then embody a new spirit
in community.

In this concluding chapter, I will examine each of these steps carefully and explore what it might mean for church leaders to have the
ears to hear what the Spirit has to say to the churches and be able
to name, call, and embody God's will and purposes in the church. I
believe that naming the spirit of a church involves an exegesis of sorts
that isn't always taught in seminary. It involves learning how to exegete
the culture of the church. In particular, I will argue that exegeting the
culture involves listening to the macro-stories and micro-stories that
have an impact on the community of faith. When we come to calling
the spirit of the church to repentance, I will focus on what it means
to read Scripture in community as a way of contrasting the spirit of
the church with the Spirit of Christ. I will conclude by looking at
what it means to begin to put a new spirit into action by embodying
Scripture together in community.

As a way of illustrating what it means to name, call, and embody
a new and life-giving spirit within the church, I will also examine the
sermon Joshua gives to the children of Israel as they prepare to enter
the promised land. I believe this sermon is an incredible model for
leaders interested in transforming a community. In this amazing communal moment, Joshua is able to find a way to name the spirit of the

community of Israel in their past and in their present, to call the spirit of the community into a new pattern of existence, and then to begin embodying God's new reality in the practices of the community.

Naming the Spirit

Learning to name the spirit of the church is a matter of learning to interpret the culture of the church. In theology, the work of interpretation is often referred to as exegesis. The telling of a people's history is not just the recitation of facts and events. It is the work of interpreting or exegeting that history as well. At some level, all of life is a text, and all texts require exegesis and interpretation. Edna St. Vincent Millay wrote a poem that expresses the need for exegesis in all of life:

> Upon this gifted age, in its dark hour,
> Rains from the sky a meteoric shower
> Of facts . . . they lie unquestioned, uncombined.
> Wisdom enough to leech us of our ill
> Is daily spun; but there exists no loom
> To weave it into fabric.[1]

Transformational leaders discover the loom to weave into a fabric of meaning the "meteoric shower of facts" and stories of a community or culture. Although there is much involved in the art of exegeting the culture, there is one practice that is essential: listening to both the macro- and the micro-stories of the community. I use the term "macro-story" to describe those narratives, events, or stories that are shared by a large portion of the culture or the community. In each of the seven letters to the churches in Asia there are macro-stories of not only the city but also of the empire of which the Revelator is keenly aware and observant. It is clear that the spirit of each church is shaped by the stories and events of its particular city and also by the influence of Rome and its history.

Transformational leaders who are interested in naming the spirits of their churches have to be aware of the macro-stories that shape the culture and community. In a media age, there are shared cultural events that cut across regions, states, and cities. Every community in

North America is deeply affected by events such as 9/11 or Hurricane Katrina. Even communities far away from New York or New Orleans in both location and culture share those events at a deep emotive level because of the images of suffering that became a common cultural memory and part of the collective national consciousness.

It is not only tragic or newsworthy events that make up the macro-stories of culture; what might be thought of as trivial events have a major influence as well. Sporting events, celebrity gossip, reality television, major motion pictures, and Internet sensations become the fodder for water-cooler conversations and shared community narratives that shape a culture's vocabulary, worldview, and collective memory. Those who want to exegete the culture can't limit their attention to the news section of the morning paper but must also pay attention to the lifestyle and entertainment sections.

The late media scholar Neil Postman used to say that advances in communication are ecological and not merely technological. Just as red dye added to a beaker of water changes the color of all the water, so too when communication technology advances, we don't have the old culture plus television or the Internet, we have a whole new culture. The leader trying to discern the macro-stories of the culture has to be aware of the impact of developments such as YouTube, Facebook, or iTunes on the shared consciousness of the culture. These global or national macro-stories and events immediately become part of the church's story.

Although there are common narratives and shared stories that impact the ethos of every congregation in North America, we are each uniquely influenced by our local settings as well. The spirit of every church I have served has been profoundly shaped by its local culture. I served on staff at a church in a small town in the Midwest that was formed when Christians who lived in the nearby large city decided that lifestyles and politics were becoming too corrupt in the big city, and so they moved just a few miles west and established what they hoped would become the model of a godly town. In an effort to ensure that the town maintained its moral fabric, rigid "blue laws"—in particular laws that banned selling liquor and forbade stores and restaurants to be open on Sundays—were established for the citizens of the town. Although the city is now well over a century old, many of the original blue laws are still in place. While our family lived there, the mayor of the town decided to paint a large blue line all the way around the city so that no matter what exit or entrance people were taking, they would know when they were entering or leaving the town. Needless to say, life "inside the blue line" was shaped by an interesting history of isolation and protectionism. Not just the church I served in but really all the churches in the town tended to be shaped either in support of or in reaction to the "Mayberry-esque" spirit that had been present since the town's inception. Like every location, this spirit gave life to certain aspects of the Christian community. For example, there was in the church a unique love for community and a sense of rallying together whenever a person or family faced hardship. But the insulated spirit of the community could also become a deadly spirit, especially in those situations when unity within the "blue line" was based on uniformity. There was a profound spirit of acceptance as long as one embraced the same values and perspectives as those living in the town. If not, one might find life inside the line to be less than hospitable.

Life in that small town was quite the opposite of life in the church I was part of during my adolescent years in Seattle. The Northwest has a free-spirited and liberal edge to it. The free-spirited ethos of Seattle meant that anybody, regardless of race, culture, or political perspective, could be accepted, but the city also fostered a highly creative and entrepreneurial spirit. During the last several decades, that area has been highly influential in the arts and in business, through such major companies as Microsoft, Boeing, Nordstrom, Eddie Bauer, Costco, and Starbucks. Each of these companies is known for being socially conscious and highly entrepreneurial. It is not surprising, then, that churches in the Northwest often find themselves wrestling to maintain boundaries of orthodoxy, on the one hand, and pushing to be entrepreneurial and to think outside the box, on the other. The church I pastored in Dallas was deeply shaped—"y'all"—by the bias toward "bigness" and "newness" that pervades that region of the Lone Star State. The church I pastor now in the Los Angeles area is in so many ways—"dude"—a reflection of the cultural, economic, and political diversity of Southern California.

The transformational leader pays attention to and learns as much as he or she can about the history and shaping stories of the local community. These macro-narratives are highly influential in the formation of the church's spirit.

But the transformational leader also learns how to interpret the micro-stories of a congregation. One of the most helpful and humorous metaphors for ministry is given by John Galloway Jr. in his book *Ministry Loves Company*. Galloway says that ministers always need to remember that they are the facilitators at somebody else's family reunion. Galloway describes pastoring as being invited to organize the reunion of a mythical family named Smythe. He writes:

> So we are arriving to pick up the ongoing enterprise of people we really do not know, in a facility we do not recognize, to lead them at a reunion whose activities they have already been practicing for years quite well without us, thank you, with well-cultivated idiosyncrasies we have never seen in our lives. In an assignment that might be called "mission impossible," they look to us to lead. To complicate our assignment, they will for a period of time accept our leadership, but only insofar as it reinforces the Smythe way of doing things, a way they refuse to make clear to us until we violate it and incur their scorn. . . . We are the facilitators at an extended family reunion in a family to which we do not belong, who have a well-developed style we have never seen, in a place we do not recognize.[2]

Because as leaders and pastors we often begin as outsiders to the community of the church, Galloway suggests that in the first year or two of ministry in a new location we focus on "compassionate, focused laziness. Just don't do much. . . . Before we have to come up with new ideas, we have time to read all the minutes of all the governing boards and committees of the church for the past five years. . . . Our present task is only to learn what is happening."[3] In other words, one of the first tasks of the transformational leader is to learn as many of the micro-stories of the community as she or he possibly can, because the stories of failure and hurt, success and blessing, and quarrels and embrace are the lifeblood of the spirit of the church.

It is clear from the opening of Joshua's sermon to the children of Israel that he has become a student of Israel's history. He begins his transformative sermon by recounting the history of Israel. As he narrates their common story, notice how he plays with the pronouns.

Then Joshua gathered all the tribes of Israel to Shechem, and summoned the elders, the heads, the judges, and the officers of Israel; and they presented themselves before God. And Joshua said to all the people, "Thus says the LORD, the God of Israel: Long ago your ancestors—Terah and his sons Abraham and Nahor—lived beyond the Euphrates and served other gods. Then I took your father Abraham from beyond the River and led him through all the land of Canaan and made his offspring many. I gave him Isaac; and to Isaac I gave Jacob and Esau. I gave Esau the hill country of Seir to possess, but Jacob and his children went down to Egypt. Then I sent Moses and Aaron, and I plagued Egypt with what I did in its midst; [here come the pronouns] and afterwards I brought *you* out. When I brought *your ancestors* out of Egypt, *you* came to the sea; and the Egyptians pursued *your ancestors* with chariots and horsemen to the Red Sea. When *they* cried out to the Lord, he put darkness between *you* and the Egyptians, and made the sea come upon *them* and cover *them*; and *your* eyes saw what I did to Egypt. Afterwards *you* lived in the wilderness a long time. (Josh. 24:1–7; emphasis added)

The genius of Joshua's sermon is its ability not only to help the children of the exodus event identify with the story of their ancestors but also to help them truly make this story their own. The story of Israel's ancestors is also the story of those who will carry it on. When Joshua leads the people into the promised land the only leaders remaining from the exodus event are Joshua and Caleb. Those who stand before Joshua that day as he rallies the people are those who have inherited the story but have not lived it personally. As Joshua recounts the significant events that so profoundly shaped the life of the people, he juxtaposes descriptions of what took place for *your ancestors* with what took place for *you*. When *our ancestors* were brought out of Egypt, *we* came to the Red Sea. When *our ancestors* cried out to the Lord, God delivered *us*. Even though those who are preparing to follow Joshua into the land were not present at the events he retells, those stories are still the life-shaping, spirit-forming narratives of the people. Those stories shape their attitudes about the present and form their vision for the future. In this great sermon, Joshua names the narratives that have formed and given life to the angel or collective spirit of the congregation of Israel.

Joshua realized that the events and stories of the ancestors of Israel weren't just their stories, they were his stories. In a mysterious way, what has happened in our city has happened to us, what is happening in our globalized media-oriented world has happened to us, and without question the stories that have shaped the life of a congregation have now happened to us. Joshua had lived with the people long enough to begin to name its spirit; one of the primary tasks for those who lead the people of God is to carefully and prayerfully learn how to name the spirit of the church formed in its macro- and micro-stories.

Calling the Spirit to Repentance

Joshua then calls the spirit of the children of Israel to repentance.

> Now therefore revere the LORD, and serve him in sincerity and in faithfulness; put away the gods that your ancestors served beyond the River and in Egypt, and serve the LORD. Now if you are unwilling to serve the LORD, choose this day whom you will serve, whether the gods your ancestors served in the region beyond the River or the gods of the Amorites in whose land you are living; but as for me and my household, we will serve the LORD. (Josh. 24:14–15)

Joshua's call for the people to repent of their idolatry and to renew their covenantal faithfulness to the Lord is formed and informed by the narratives of covenant found throughout the Torah. In particular, the words of commitment in Joshua 24 reflect the call in the Shema to "love the LORD your God with all your heart, and with all your soul, and with all your might" (Deut. 6:5). Transforming the spirit of a church takes place inasmuch as we allow Scripture to interpret the nature of the community's life together. I would suggest that we discover what it means to call the spirit of the church to repentance as we learn to read Scripture well in community.[4]

Learning (or relearning) to read Scripture in community implies first of all that the reading of Scripture creates a unique group of people. Scripture calls this sacred community by various names: "a chosen race, a royal priesthood, a holy nation, God's own people" (1 Pet. 2:9). The purpose of reading Scripture in this kind of community is not to gain a storehouse of biblical data but to train our spiritual eyes to discern together the presence of God in the world. In other words, we read Scripture in community to learn to interpret ourselves and the world as Christians. For the community of faith, Scripture becomes a set of glasses through which we view not only the world but also our lives and the life of the community. To borrow Millay's image, the revelation of God in Christ through Scripture becomes the loom on which we weave the data, facts, and events of the world into a fabric.

To put it very simply, each time the community gathers around Scripture, we are holding up the revelation of God's character as a contrast model to our own. In the Old Testament, God's steadfast covenantal love and mercy are held up in contrast to the people's self-centeredness and unfaithfulness. When the character of God's people is called into question, it is not compared with the character of the nations surrounding Israel but rather held in contrast to the God whose nature they are called to embody and represent in the world. In the New Testament, the character of contrast is obviously that of Christ Jesus. Every time we read the Gospels together as a community we are in essence being asked to look at Jesus, then look at ourselves, and confess the great difference.

Interestingly, it is finally the voice of Christ that speaks through the Revelator in the seven letters. He is the one who "holds the seven stars in his right hand, who walks among the seven golden lampstands" (Rev. 2:1). He is the one who gives "permission to eat from the tree of life that is in the paradise of God" (2:7). He is the "first and the last, who was dead and came to life" (2:8). It is Christ who "has the sharp two-edged sword" (2:12). It is he who has "eyes like a flame of fire, and whose feet are like burnished bronze" (2:18). Jesus "has the seven spirits of God and the seven stars" (3:1). He alone is "the holy one, the true one, who has the key of David, who opens and no one will shut, who shuts and no one opens" (3:7). He is the "amen, the faithful and true witness, the origin of God's creation" (3:14). Christ stands at the door and knocks (3:20).

Each of the letters begins and ends with Christ. In him we see the fullness of who God is, but we also see who, by God's grace, we might become. The deadly spirits of the churches are only healed as they are confronted and contrasted with the image of God in Christ that we discover in Scripture. For this reason leaders must be careful not to be so quick to look for narratives that defend the status quo of the community; rather, they should allow the reading and preaching of Scripture to truthfully judge the community of faith in the light of the character of Christ.

There are certain virtues necessary to read Scripture in community well. The Revelator in each letter writes that it takes "an ear to listen to what the Spirit is saying." A people who is combative, frightened, and exclusive can never read the Scriptures in community. A community capable of hearing what the Spirit is saying to the churches must have a deep faith or conviction that the pursuit of a truthful reading and hearing of the Word is not destructive to God or to God's people. Honesty becomes a necessity for being able to read Scripture faithfully in community. Honesty in the church means at the very least that one can tell the truth in the body about our lives and the world. Honesty does not mean a lack of disagreement, but it does mean that it is possible to speak the truth in love for the sake of building up the body of Christ.

Embodying a New Spirit in Practice

The community of faith must have the ears to hear what the Spirit is saying to the churches by hearing the Scriptures in community, but the redeeming of the deadly spirit of a church can only fully be achieved as we also learn to *embody* the Scriptures in community. As we embody Scripture we allow a new spirit to be put into practice. After Joshua names the spirit of the children of Israel and calls that spirit to repentance, he awaits the response of the people.

> Then the people answered, "Far be it from us that we should forsake the LORD to serve other gods; for it is the LORD our God who brought *us and our ancestors* up from the land of Egypt, out of the house of slavery, and who did those great signs in our sight. He protected us along the way that we went, and among all the peoples through whom we passed; and the LORD drove out before us all the peoples, the Amorites who lived in the land. Therefore we also will serve the LORD, for he is our God. (Josh. 24:16–18; emphasis added)

There are a couple of things that I find fascinating about the response of the people here. First, I love that they grasp the way in which their story is intertwined with the story they inherited. Joshua had worked so hard at playing with the pronouns in an attempt to help the people identify not only their current situation but also how their lives were caught up in the story and spirit of those who came before them. They do seem to "get it" because they respond to Joshua that they will indeed follow God because it is he who brought "*us and our ancestors*" up from the land of Egypt. Embodying Scripture begins by accepting our story and God's story as our own. When our ancestors were delivered, we were delivered. And when our ancestors were unfaithful, we were unfaithful. They begin to find a new spirit by accepting all that has gone before and committing their ways afresh to God.

After they commit to God's purposes and intentions, Joshua puts them to work: "He said, 'Then put away the foreign gods that are among you, and incline your hearts to the LORD, the God of Israel'" (24:23). He also set up a stone to witness to the renewed covenantal commitment the people had made to God (24:26).

Transforming the spirits of the churches requires more than hearing, confessing, and committing. It involves a new set of actions. The Revelator calls each of the seven churches to listen and to conquer. How does the church conquer? I believe that it involves embodying Scripture in community. To do this requires more than just asking what Jesus would do; it is about forming together as a community the dispositions and virtues that make it possible for us to embody the proper spirit of Christ in the world.

I am part of the VCR generation, which means I grew up renting great movies from the 80s for Friday-night parties. One of my favorite films from the VCR era is *The Karate Kid*. In the film, Ralph Macchio plays Daniel Larusso, a young adolescent who is struggling with love, life, and especially getting beaten up by a pack of teenage karate experts. In search of help and a father figure, Daniel discovers Mr. Miyagi—a Yoda-like neighbor played by Pat Morita—when Mr. Miyagi rescues him from yet another beating by the town bullies. Having demonstrated his surprising expertise in the martial arts while rescuing Daniel, Mr. Miyagi becomes both a friend and a karate tutor for the young boy so that Daniel can learn to defend himself against his enemies.

The classic scene from the movie is when Daniel shows up for his first lesson in karate and Mr. Miyagi assigns him to wax his car. Mr. Miyagi shows him the exact method of putting the "Wax on! Wax off! Wax on! Wax off!" Tired, confused, and frustrated, Daniel returns the next day hoping to now be taught karate but instead is again put to work, this time sanding the deck. One more time Daniel comes for his lessons only this time to be put to work painting the fence. Finally at the end of his rope, and quite convinced that he is simply being used as some form of forced labor, he gets very angry with Mr. Miyagi and proceeds to tell him off. His tirade is interrupted when Mr. Miyagi tries to throw a punch at him but Daniel easily deflects it with a "Wax on! Wax off!" motion of his arm. In that moment Mr. Miyagi reveals to Daniel that the repetitious muscle motions he has learned after three days of waxing the car, sanding the deck, and painting the fence are the very instinctive muscles that needed to be trained in order to become a great martial artist.

I don't believe that we can secretly and subversively transform the deadly spirits of the church through having the pastor's car waxed—although I am willing to give this a try—but I do believe that the destructive spirits of the church come to us through embodied practices of a destructive kind. So in contrast, life-giving spirits can be renewed in us only by learning new sets of practices together as a community of faith. We all need to have our spiritual muscles, which seem to respond so easily to sin, retrained to participate in the will of God for his church.

I come from the Holiness tradition, which historically has emphasized the renewal of all of life. When we have failed as a tradition, in my opinion, it has not been in having an overly optimistic view of God's transforming grace but in believing that transformation takes place primarily through individual commitment and willpower. Don't misunderstand me. There is an important place for hearing the call to repentance and holy living and then committing ourselves to it, but we must not only hear the Word, we must do it. I believe it is practices—and in particular spiritual practices done in Christian community—that help to make us complete in Christ.

If we go back to the seven deadly spirits we discovered in the letters to the Asian churches, perhaps we can begin to imagine the embodied practices that the churches need to discover in order to retrain their spiritual muscles.

Perhaps the boundary keepers of Ephesus could rediscover the spiritual practices of mercy. As the Ephesians reach out to those existing at the margins of society, they will discover anew that the church becomes less divisive over issues when those issues cease to be simply theoretical and begin to have names and people attached to them. In my own context, works of mercy have helped us as a church to realize that it is one thing to have a view on what should happen to undocumented workers and quite another to have opinions on what should happen to our friends Jesse or Esther.

The spirit of consumerism is not only named but also transformed through disciplines of simplicity and giving. Many of the people who attend my church make their living in one way or another in connection to the entertainment industry. Every form of entertainment is done with quality and excellence. Here in Pasadena we are not just known for having a parade, we are known for having the "Grandaddy of them all." I often feel the pressure of consumerism carry over into worship. Like the movie critics Ebert and Roeper, many people who worship with our church each week are critiquing everything—from the parking and the announcements to the music and the preaching—with a thumbs-up or thumbs-down. I know of many churches that hire "service producers" to ensure that the worship service runs smoothly and professionally. In our world, it is very easy to turn God into another product to market and consume. The church possessed by the spirit of consumption and consumerism has to retrain the spiritual muscles that take and receive to give and let go.

Pergamum's spirit of accommodation, especially accommodation to power, is met and transformed through participation with the sacramental symbols of broken body and shed blood. I was recently reminded of the contrast of symbols between the empire and the church while attending an Independence Day parade. The symbols in the parade were all symbols of political power and conquest: planes, jeeps, tanks, weapons, and flags. After the parade, I went to the church to set up for a communion service. I was struck by the symbols of

Christian worship: the towel and basin, the cross as a means of execution, and the elements of the Lord's Supper, which are reminders of sacrifice. In a world (and church) accommodated to power, we need to participate all the more in the inverted symbols of Christ's upside-down kingdom.[5]

Privatized faith in Thyatira can be changed through the discipline of confession within a community of care. John Wesley's small-group meetings often began with each person answering the question, "How have you sinned since the last time we got together?" I've often thought that prayer meetings and small groups might be a lot more exciting and a lot more intimate if we started with this question.

The apathetic faith of Sardis meets its match in disciplines of sacrifice and what Dallas Willard calls the discipline of secrecy (doing good deeds without receiving credit).[6] In *The Three Christs of Ypsilanti*, psychologist Milton Rokeach writes about Leon, Joseph, and Clyde, three chronic psychiatric patients each suffering from a messiah complex. Each one maintained that he was the reincarnation of Jesus Christ. When Rokeach put them in a recovery group together, some interesting conversations ensued: "One of the men would claim, 'I'm the messiah, the Son of God. I am on a mission. I was sent here to save the earth.' 'How do you know?' Rokeach would ask. 'God told me.' And one of the other patients would counter, 'I never told you any such thing.'"[7] Commenting about this experiment, John Ortberg writes, "The bitter irony is, the very delusion to which they clung so tenaciously is what cut them off from life. . . . If you want to be your own god, you have to settle for living in a tiny universe where there is room for only one person. Your world could grow infinitely bigger if you were only willing to become . . . appropriately small."[8] Apathetic faith is the by-product of a worldview that has become too small. Humility and service allow us to expand our understanding of the needs in the world and thus of our need for larger faith.

A spirit of fear is overcome by the power of communal prayer. Later in John's apocalyptic vision there is a great moment in which "there was silence in heaven for about half an hour" (Rev. 8:1). In the midst of seals being opened and trumpets of judgment sounding, John has a vision of heaven being completely still so that God can receive "the prayers of all the saints on the gold altar that is before the throne"

(8:3). The prayers of the saints are then mixed with the fire from the altar and thrown back to earth, creating "peals of thunder, rumblings, flashes of lightning, and an earthquake" (8:5). Eugene Peterson refers to this moment as "reversed thunder." Faced with insurmountable challenges, the early Christians "had neither weapons nor votes. They had little money and no prestige. Why didn't they have mental breakdowns? Why didn't they cut and run? They prayed. . . . The prayers which had ascended, unremarked by journalists of the day, returned with immense force . . . as 'reversed thunder.'"[9] Prayer allows the church to tap into the grace and presence of God already at work in the world, and like the Christians of Philadelphia, helps us to see the challenges we often fear as open doors for God to work.

The self-sufficient spirit of Laodicea begins to find renewal in disciplines of dependency, such as fasting and waiting on the Lord. We become self-sufficient when we are fooled into believing that our lives and the way things are now are the way things always will be. Disciplines such as fasting allow us to break our daily routines so that we are sensitized to those who are left outside the system. Such disciplines also remind us that we have learned dependency on our stomachs and our appetites rather than on God.

Although naming the spirit of the church and calling the spirit to repentance through the lens of the Scripture are critical first steps, full transformation takes place only as we learn to embody these practices of faith as a means of restorative and transformative grace.

This is without question both a wonderful and difficult time to be a follower of Christ. There are pressures on church leaders to grow, to entertain, to administrate, to counsel, to challenge, to build, and a hundred other tasks. Each of those is important in its own way. I am, however, increasingly convinced that those who are leaders in the church have a responsibility to discern the spirit of the church. This "angel" of the church, formed in mysterious ways from our life together in community, can give life (as it was doing in Smyrna and Philadelphia), or it can be deadly (as it was in Ephesus, Pergamum, Thyatira, Sardis, and Laodicea). Discerning the spirit takes patience, grace, vulnerability, and godly wisdom, but like the Revelator, our task is to speak for the Lord of the church and call the deadly spirits of the church to obedience to the Father. The good news for the church today is not that we are free from the spirits of boundary keeping, consumerism, accommodation, privatized faith, apathetic faith, fear, or self-sufficiency but that we rest in the fact that the Lord reproves and disciplines only those he loves. As he did for the church in Laodicea, the Lord continues to do for us. He stands at the door and knocks, inviting us to be open to his renewed life with us. Let anyone who has an ear listen to what the Spirit is saying to the churches.

Questions for Group Discussion

1. What are some of the things that need to take place in order for a transformational leader to be able to name the spirit of a congregation?
2. What are some of the macro-stories that have most profoundly shaped the spirit of your church?
3. What are some of the micro-stories that have most profoundly shaped the spirit of your church?
4. Are there any biblical narratives that serve as sharp contrast models for what your church is now and what Christ wants it to be as his body in the world?
5. What actions or practices can the community of faith begin to participate in that might shape the spirit of the congregation more toward Christ's vision for the church?

Notes

Introduction

1. Hendrikus Berkhof, *Christ and the Powers* (Scottdale, PA: Herald, 1977).

2. Walter Wink, *Naming the Powers: The Language of Power in the New Testament* (Philadelphia: Fortress, 1984); *Unmasking the Powers: The Invisible Powers That Determine Human Existence* (Philadelphia: Fortress, 1986); *Engaging the Powers: Discernment and Resistance in a World of Domination* (Philadelphia: Fortress, 1992); *When the Powers Fall: Reconciliation in the Healing of the Nations* (Philadelphia: Fortress, 1998).

3. See Warren S. Brown, Nancey Murphy, and H. Newton Malony, eds., *Whatever Happened to the Soul? Scientific and Theological Portraits of Human Nature* (Minneapolis: Fortress, 1998), 127–48.

4. I realize there is much debate regarding the authorship of the Revelation, but for the sake of this work, I am making the assumption that the tradition that holds John "the Beloved" as the author of Revelation is correct. I will also treat the work as the creation of a single author writing in exile from the Isle of Patmos, even though I am aware that this too is a matter of scholarly debate.

5. For those interested in learning to read Revelation as a social critique of empire, I highly recommend Wes Howard-Brook and Anthony Gwyther, *Unveiling Empire: Reading Revelation Then and Now* (Maryknoll, NY: Orbis Books, 2001).

6. Craig R. Koester, *Revelation and the End of All Things* (Grand Rapids: Eerdmans, 2001), 56.

7. See Bruce M. Metzger, *Breaking the Code: Understanding the Book of Revelation* (Nashville: Abingdon, 1993), 30; Koester, *Revelation*, 56; Colin J. Hemer, *The Letters to the Seven Churches of Asia in Their Local Setting* (Grand Rapids: Eerdmans, 1986), 32; George Eldon Ladd, *A Commentary on the Revelation of John* (Grand Rapids: Eerdmans, 1972), 35; Darrell W. Johnson, *Discipleship on the Edge:*

143

An Expository Journey through the Book of Revelation (Vancouver: Regent College Publishing, 2004), 51.

8. See Catherine Gunsalus Gonzalez and Justo L. Gonzalez, *Westminster Bible Companion: Revelation* (Louisville: Westminster John Knox, 1997), 20; Ladd, *Revelation of John*, 35; and Koester, *Revelation*, 56.

9. Again see Metzger, *Breaking the Code*, 30; Koester, *Revelation*, 56; Hemer, *Letters to the Seven Churches*, 32; Ladd, *Revelation of John*, 35; and Johnson, *Discipleship on the Edge*, 51.

10. Wink, *Unmasking the Powers*, 70; Gonzalez and Gonzalez, *Revelation*, 20.

11. Wink, *Unmasking the Powers*, 70.

12. See Johnson, *Discipleship on the Edge*, 51–52.

13. Walter Rauschenbusch makes a similar argument about the corporate spiritual essence of a community. He refers to these spirits as "super-personal forces." See Rauschenbusch, *A Theology for the Social Gospel* (Nashville: Abingdon, 1917), 69–76.

14. For descriptions of emergentist theory of human personhood, see Nancey Murphy, *Bodies and Souls, or Spirited Bodies?* (Cambridge: Cambridge University Press, 2006); Brown, Murphy, and Malony, *Whatever Happened to the Soul?*; Joel B. Green and Stuart L. Palmer, *In Search of the Soul: Four Views of the Mind-Body Problem* (Downers Grove, IL: InterVarsity, 2005).

15. William Hasker, "On Behalf of Emergent Dualism," in Green and Palmer, *In Search of the Soul*, 75.

16. Ibid.

17. Ibid.

18. Ibid., 76.

19. Wink, *Unmasking the Powers*, 71, 73.

20. See ibid., 73–77.

21. Ibid., 76–77.

22. This is also a likely reason that the "mark of the beast" is the number 666. Those who participate in the life of the beast, or are servants of the beast, are marked in such a way that their lives will always add up to incompleteness. It is possible that the mark is also a reference to the weight of Solomon's gold. "The weight of the gold that came to Solomon in one year was six hundred sixty-six talents of gold" (1 Kings 10:14). Even if it is a reference to Solomon's gold, the symbolism is the same. In the same way Solomon destroyed the fabric and unity of the kingdom by pursuing wealth and power (on the backs of slave labor), so too the empire in Revelation (Babylon) marks people by pulling them into a way of life that always is unsatisfying at best and utterly destructive at worst.

Chapter 1 Ephesus

1. William M. Ramsay, *The Letters to the Seven Churches* (Grand Rapids: Baker Academic, 1985), 238.

2. Robert H. Mounce, *Revelation*, New International Commentary on the New Testament (Grand Rapids: Eerdmans, 1997), 67.

3. In 29 BCE; in 90 CE, the temple to Domitian, later changed for Vespasian; and to Hadrian in 190 CE. See Darrell W. Johnson, *Discipleship on the Edge: An*

Expository Journey through the Book of Revelation (Vancouver: Regent College Publishing, 2004), 54.

4. Ramsay, *Letters to the Seven Churches*, 245.

5. Ibid., 239.

6. Ignatius, *To the Ephesians* 6, in *The Apostolic Fathers in English*, trans. and ed. Michael Holmes, 3rd ed. (Grand Rapids: Baker Academic, 2006), 88.

7. See Koester, *Revelation*, 58, and William Barclay, *Letters to the Seven Churches* (Louisville: Westminster John Knox, 2001), 13.

8. Barclay, *Letters to the Seven Churches*, 13.

9. Mounce, *Revelation*, 69.

10. Barclay, *Letters to the Seven Churches*, 11.

11. Catherine Gunsalus Gonzalez and Justo L. Gonzalez, *Westminster Bible Companion: Revelation* (Louisville: Westminster John Knox, 1997), 24.

12. See Earl F. Palmer, *1, 2, 3 John, Revelation*, The Communicator's Commentary (Waco, TX: Word Books, 1982), 129.

13. See Hans Frei, "Response to 'Narrative Theology: An Evangelical Appraisal,'" *Trinity Journal* 8 (Spring 1987): 21–24. Narrative theology is a twentieth-century movement that emphasizes presenting the faith by using the narrative nature of the biblical text rather than using the Bible to create highly propositional systematic theologies.

14. See Stanley J. Grenz, *Renewing the Center: Evangelical Theology in a Post-Theological Era* (Grand Rapids: Baker Academic, 2000), 325.

15. See Nancey Murphy, *Beyond Liberalism and Fundamentalism: How Modern and Postmodern Philosophy Set the Theological Agenda* (Valley Forge, PA: Trinity Press International, 1996); Grenz, *Renewing the Center*; Brian D. McLaren, *A Generous Orthodoxy: Why I Am a Missional, Evangelical, Post/Protestant, Liberal/Conservative, Mystical/Poetic, Biblical, Charismatic/Contemplative, Fundamentalist/Calvinist, Anabaptist/Anglican, Methodist, Catholic, Green, Incarnational, Depressed-Yet-Hopeful, Emergent, Unfinished Christian* (Grand Rapids: Zondervan, 2004).

16. Murphy, *Beyond Liberalism and Fundamentalism*, 154.

17. Grenz, *Renewing the Center*, 325.

18. Ibid., 321.

19. McLaren, *Generous Orthodoxy*, 21.

20. Ibid., 30–31.

Chapter 2 Smyrna

1. Jonathan Allen, "The Disney Touch at a Hindu Temple," *New York Times*, June 8, 2006, http://travel2.nytimes.com/2006/06/08/travel/08letter.html?pagewanted=1&e i=5070&en=902afb499ae75c2f&ex=1149998400 (accessed June 17, 2008).

2. Ibid.

3. Ibid.

4. In my own denomination—the Church of the Nazarene—over the last twenty years the number of worshipers in North America has remained almost the same, but over that same period of time the number of churches with over one thousand in attendance has gone from three to well over thirty. *The Christian Science Monitor* reports that a survey by researchers at Hartford Seminary in Connecticut and Leadership Network in Dallas revealed that the number of megachurches (churches

with weekly attendance over 2000) doubled between 2001 and 2006 (Jane Lampman, "Worship Is on the Rise," *The Christian Science Monitor*, February 6, 2006, www .csmonitor.com/2006/0206/p13s01-lire.html [accessed August 26, 2008]).

5. See Catherine Gunsalus Gonzalez and Justo L. Gonzalez, *Westminster Bible Companion: Revelation* (Louisville: Westminster John Knox, 1997), 25.

6. Colin J. Hemer, *The Letters to the Seven Churches of Asia in Their Local Setting* (Grand Rapids: Eerdmans, 1986), 58.

7. See Gonzalez and Gonzalez, *Revelation*, 26.

8. William Barclay, *Letters to the Seven Churches* (Louisville: Westminster John Knox, 2001), 17.

9. Ibid.

10. George Eldon Ladd, *A Commentary on the Revelation of John* (Grand Rapids: Eerdmans, 1972), 42.

11. It is also possible that the "ten days" refers back to the time when Daniel, Hananiah, Mishael, and Azariah were tested for ten days after they refused to eat the defiling food of Nebuchadnezzar (Dan. 1:12).

12. See Darrell W. Johnson, *Discipleship on the Edge: An Expository Journey through the Book of Revelation* (Vancouver: Regent College Publishing, 2004), 73–74.

13. See Robert N. Bellah et al., *Habits of the Heart: Individualism and Commitment in American Life* (Berkeley: University of California Press, 1985), 27–31.

14. Ibid., viii.

15. Ibid., ix.

16. Ibid.

17. Ibid.

18. Ibid., 153.

19. See ibid., 155–62.

20. Ibid., 144.

21. Michael W. Holmes, trans. and ed., *The Apostolic Fathers in English*, 3rd ed. (Grand Rapids: Baker Academic, 2006), 142.

22. *The Martyrdom of Polycarp* 3, 9–10, in Holmes, *Apostolic Fathers*, 148, 150–51.

23. *The Martyrdom of Polycarp* 15, in Holmes, *Apostolic Fathers*, 153.

Chapter 3 Pergamum

1. See for example Wes Howard-Brook and Anthony Gwyther, *Unveiling Empire: Reading Revelation Then and Now* (Maryknoll, NY: Orbis Books, 2001).

2. George Eldon Ladd, *A Commentary on the Revelation of John* (Grand Rapids: Eerdmans, 1972), 45.

3. "Food sacrificed to idols" can refer "to meat purchased in the public market which had formerly been sacrificed in a pagan temple and later sold to the market, or it can refer to feasts conducted in the temples in honor of various gods. The problem of these meats which Christians must buy in the public market had arisen in Corinth, and Paul dealt with it at length, declaring that nothing is unclean of itself, and that unless it is offensive to a man's conscience, he does no wrong in eating such meat (1 Cor. 7:7–13). At the same time, Paul says that it is impossible to drink the cup of the Lord and the cup of demons (1 Cor. 10:21), and in this case he must have

reference to actual participation in temple feasts which amounted to worship of the deity involved. Such seems to be the situation in Pergamum. It would be difficult to understand this prohibition as a restriction against buying meat in the open market; rather, it refers to active participation in feasts in the temples in honor of the pagan deities" (Ladd, *Revelation of John*, 47).

4. Bruce W. Longenecker, *The Lost Letters of Pergamum* (Grand Rapids: Baker Academic, 2003).

5. Ibid., 177.

6. For a fascinating description of Solomon as the embodiment of "empire" and as Israel's version of Pharaoh, see Walter Brueggemann, *Mandate to Difference: An Invitation to the Contemporary Church* (Louisville: Westminster John Knox, 2007), 16–26.

Chapter 4 Thyatira

1. Steve Springer, "Eli's Not Coming: Former BYU Lineman Herring Has the Ability to Play in the NFL, but It's Never on Sunday for This Mormon," *Los Angeles Times*, September 15, 1995, 1.

2. Ibid.

3. See William M. Ramsay, *The Letters to the Seven Churches* (Grand Rapids: Baker Academic, 1985), 325.

4. Darrell W. Johnson, *Discipleship on the Edge: An Expository Journey through the Book of Revelation* (Vancouver: Regent College Publishing, 2004), 87.

5. Ramsay, *Letters to the Seven Churches*, 344.

6. William Barclay, *Letters to the Seven Churches* (Louisville: Westminster John Knox, 2001), 47.

7. Ibid., 52.

8. Ibid., 49.

9. Ibid., 55.

10. For a recent and excellent description of the Hebraic view of the unity of the body, see N. T. Wright, *Surprised by Hope: Rethinking Heaven, the Resurrection, and the Mission of the Church* (San Francisco: HarperOne, 2008).

11. See William R. Herzog II, *Parables as Subversive Speech: Jesus as Pedagogue of the Oppressed* (Louisville: Westminster John Knox, 1994), 150–70.

Chapter 5 Sardis

1. See Robert H. Mounce, *Revelation*, New International Commentary on the New Testament (Grand Rapids: Eerdmans, 1997), 93–94.

2. William M. Ramsay, *The Letters to the Seven Churches* (Grand Rapids: Baker Academic, 1985), 354.

3. Catherine Gunsalus Gonzalez and Justo L. Gonzalez, *Westminster Bible Companion: Revelation* (Louisville: Westminster John Knox, 1997), 32.

4. George Eldon Ladd, *A Commentary on the Revelation of John* (Grand Rapids: Eerdmans, 1972), 56.

5. Ramsay, *Letters to the Seven Churches*, 380.

6. William Barclay, *Letters to the Seven Churches* (Louisville: Westminster John Knox, 2001), 59.

7. As quoted in Darrell W. Johnson, *Discipleship on the Edge: An Expository Journey through the Book of Revelation* (Vancouver: Regent College Publishing, 2004), 98.

8. Craig R. Koester, *Revelation and the End of All Things* (Grand Rapids: Eerdmans, 2001), 67.

9. Reggie McNeal, *The Present Future: Six Tough Questions for the Church* (San Francisco: Jossey-Bass, 2003), 15–16.

10. Ibid., 11–12.

11. Ibid., 28, 42.

12. A recent study that I highly recommend is David T. Olson, *The American Church in Crisis: Groundbreaking Research Based on a National Database of over 200,000 Churches* (Grand Rapids: Zondervan, 2008).

13. See McNeal, *Present Future*, 4.

14. Ibid., 52.

15. See Colin J. Hemer, *The Letters to the Seven Churches of Asia in Their Local Setting* (Grand Rapids: Eerdmans, 1986), 151.

16. Ramsay, *Letters to the Seven Churches*, 390.

Chapter 6 Philadelphia

1. See Robert H. Mounce, *Revelation*, New International Commentary on the New Testament (Grand Rapids: Eerdmans, 1997), 99.

2. Darrell W. Johnson, *Discipleship on the Edge: An Expository Journey through the Book of Revelation* (Vancouver: Regent College Publishing, 2004), 107.

3. William M. Ramsay, *The Letters to the Seven Churches* (Grand Rapids: Baker Academic, 1985), 397.

4. Mounce, *Revelation*, 101.

5. Ramsay, *Letters to the Seven Churches*, 411.

6. Ibid.

7. Craig R. Koester, *Revelation and the End of All Things* (Grand Rapids: Eerdmans, 2001), 66.

8. Johnson, *Discipleship on the Edge*, 111–12.

9. George Barna, *The Second Coming of the Church* (Nashville: Word, 1998), 2.

10. For a good recent model of ministry that embraces ethnic diversity, see Mark Deymaz, *Building a Healthy Multi-Ethnic Church: Mandate, Commitments, and Practices of a Diverse Congregation* (San Francisco: Jossey-Bass, 2007).

11. Barna, *Second Coming of the Church*, 3.

12. Ibid., 66.

13. William Barclay, *Letters to the Seven Churches* (Louisville: Westminster John Knox, 2001), 70.

Chapter 7 Laodicea

1. William M. Ramsay, *The Letters to the Seven Churches* (Grand Rapids: Baker Academic, 1985), 422.

2. See Robert H. Mounce, *Revelation*, New International Commentary on the New Testament (Grand Rapids: Eerdmans, 1997), 108.

3. George Eldon Ladd, *A Commentary on the Revelation of John* (Grand Rapids: Eerdmans, 1972), 64.

4. Quoted in William Barclay, *Letters to the Seven Churches* (Louisville: Westminster John Knox, 2001), 81.

5. Darrell W. Johnson, *Discipleship on the Edge: An Expository Journey through the Book of Revelation* (Vancouver: Regent College Publishing, 2004), 122.

6. Ladd, *Revelation of John*, 66.

7. Jacques Ellul, *The Meaning of the City* (Grand Rapids: Eerdmans, 1970), 5, cited in Johnson, *Discipleship on the Edge*, 123.

8. Luke Tyerman, *The Life and Times of John Wesley, M.A. Founder of the Methodists*, vol. 3 (London: Hodder and Stoughton, 1871), 520.

Chapter 8 The Ears to Hear

1. Edna St. Vincent Millay, *Huntsman, What Quarry?* as quoted in Neil Postman, *Building a Bridge to the 18th Century: How the Past Can Improve Our Future* (New York: Vintage Books, 1999), 9.

2. John Galloway Jr., *Ministry Loves Company: A Survival Guide for Pastors* (Louisville: Westminster John Knox, 2003), 10.

3. Ibid., 15–16.

4. I want to thank Dr. Stephen Green for his help in formulating these final two categories. In particular Steve's unpublished paper titled "A Holy Church" has been very helpful for me in thinking through the various ways that Scripture shapes the church's life in community.

5. For a powerful discussion of political symbols in contrast to kingdom of God symbols, see Shane Claiborne and Chris Haw, *Jesus for President* (Grand Rapids: Zondervan, 2008); and Gregory A. Boyd, *The Myth of a Christian Nation: How the Quest for Political Power Is Destroying the Church* (Grand Rapids: Zondervan, 2005).

6. See Dallas Willard, *The Spirit of the Disciplines: Understanding How God Changes Lives* (San Francisco: HarperSanFrancisco, 1988), 172–74.

7. John Ortberg, *The Life You've Always Wanted: Spiritual Disciplines for Ordinary People* (Grand Rapids: Zondervan, 2002), 108, citing Milton Rokeach, *The Three Christs of Ypsilanti* (New York: Knopf, 1964).

8. Ibid., 108–9.

9. Eugene H. Peterson, *Reversed Thunder: The Revelation of John and the Praying Imagination* (San Francisco: HarperSanFrancisco, 1988), 87–88.

Scripture Index

Subject Index